Fidel

A Story of Love and Loss

A Play in Two Acts by

Louis E.V. Nevaer

FIDEL: A STORY OF LOVE AND LOSS

Copyright 2017 by Louis E.V. Nevaer

All Rights Reserved
International Copyright Secured

No part of this work may be reproduced in any form or by any means, electronic or mechanical, including photocopying, recording, or by an information storage and retrieval system, without written permission in writing from the Publisher. Unauthorized copying, adapting, recording or public performance is an infringement of copyright.
Infringers are liable
under the law.

Publication date: February 2017
ISBN 978-1-939879-16-5

Contact publisher for additional copies and performance rights information:

Ediciones del Mayab
Calle 59 #572 x 72 & 74
Colonia Centro
Mérida, Yucatán
Mexico

Email: *info@hispaniceconomics.com*

Cover and interior design by John Clifton
johnclifton.net

DEDICATION

Lía Cámara Blum

Fidel

SYNOPSIS

Exiled to Mexico, Fidel Castro plots—along with his brother Raúl and Ernesto "Che" Guevara—to overthrow the government of Cuban dictator Fulgencio Batista. What Fidel does not anticipate is falling in love with a Mexican school teacher, Lía Cámara. He must, however, abandon her to wage revolution in Cuba. Months after consolidating power, he sends for her. She flies to Havana and is received as a dignitary. She tours Cuba and decides to stay, where she throws herself in establishing a rural school system to bring literacy to millions of Cuban peasants. In short order, however, she begins to have misgiving as the Revolution takes a dark, totalitarian turn. Torn between her love for Fidel, who has asked her to marry him and become the First Lady of Cuba, and her convictions, she abruptly decides to leave Cuba. Heartbroken, Fidel goes about his Revolution—lashing out with anger and terror against his political opponents—but across the decades, the former lovers remain very much in each other's minds—and hearts. The last contact takes place in November 2015, a year before he died at the age of 90.

Time: 1955-1961

Place: Cuba and Mexico, various locales.

CAST OF CHARACTERS

FIDEL CASTRO, Cuban revolutionary leader, age 29-35.

LÍA CÁMARA, Mexican school teacher, age 20-26.

PEDRO CÁMARA LARA, mid-50s. father of Lía Cámara.

SOCORRO BLUM DE CÁMARA, early-50s, mother of Lía Cámara.

RAÚL CASTRO, brother of Fidel and Cuban revolutionary, age 24-30.

ERNESTO "CHE" GUEVARA, Argentine sociopath and revolutionary, age 27-33.

GILBERTO BOSQUES, 60s, Mexico's ambassador to Cuba.

GUARD, 20s, first appears as a jailer for the Batista government, then he appears as a Revolutionary *barbudo*, and, finally, as official of the Cuban Consulate.

SYNOPSIS OF SCENES

Act I

Scene 1 -	A prison cell	1
Scene 2 -	The Cámara Living Room	4
Scene 3 -	A small apartment in Mexico City	9
Scene 4 -	Interior of a bus	15
Scene 5 -	The apartment in Mexico City	29
Scene 6 -	The Cámara Residence	34
Scene 7 -	The Cámara Residence	43
Scene 8 -	The apartment in Mexico City	52
Scene 9 -	The Cámara Residence	55

Act II

Scene 1 - The Cámara Residence	57
Scene 2 - A balcony overlooking a plaza	60
Scene 3 - An office in Havana	61
Scene 4 - The balcony	67
Scene 5 - The Cámara Residence	70
Scene 6 - A schoolroom	80
Scene 7 - The Mexican Embassy in Havana	87
Scene 8 - An office in Havana	90
Scene 9 - The Mexican Embassy	95
Scene 10 - The office in Havana	101
Scene 11 - The Cámara Residence	103

Epilogue - The Cámara Residence, 54 years later   108

Act I

Scene 1

Havana, Cuba. 1955

FIDEL CASTRO *is seated on the floor of a prison cell. He looks down, dejected. A* GUARD, *wearing a military uniform, appears at the bars. The* GUARD *is carrying a small suitcase that he places on the floor next to him. He is accompanied by a well-dressed man,* GILBERTO BOSQUES, *who is holding a folder with papers, and a fedora. The* GUARD *uses a baton to make noise on the bars.*

GUARD: *(Sarcastically)* Today's your lucky day.
FIDEL: *(Looking up)* What?
GUARD: You heard me. Today's your lucky day.
FIDEL: *(Standing up)* What do you mean?
GUARD: *(With arrogance)* Your ex-wife. Her family pulled strings and got the president to grant you amnesty.
FIDEL: *(Suddenly anxious)* Amnesty?
GUARD: That's right. Amnesty.
FIDEL: I'm free to go?
GUARD: Amnesty is not the same thing as being free to go.
FIDEL: What do you mean? *(Looking at the* GUARD *and then at* BOSQUES*)* This is a trick. I refuse to leave this cell if I am not at unconditional liberty.
GUARD: You cannot stay in this cell. President's orders. And you don't have a say.
FIDEL: *(Adamant)* I REFUSE TO LEAVE.
GUARD: *(In a loud, forceful voice)* The prisoner has two choices. The prisoner either accepts amnesty—and the terms under which it is granted—or the prisoner refuses amnesty, in which case, the prisoner will be marched off to the *paredón*.
FIDEL: The *paredón?*
GUARD: Yes, the firing squad. *(Pause)* It's up to the prisoner

to make his choice: the firing squad or . . . *(pointing to* BOSQUES*) amnesty.*
FIDEL: Who's this man?
BOSQUES: Mr. Castro, allow me to introduce myself. I am Gilberto Bosques—
GUARD: —Ambassador Bosques.
FIDEL: Ambassador?
BOSQUES: Mexico, at Cuba's request, has granted you political asylum.
FIDEL: Asylum? *(Pause)* I refuse.
GUARD: *(Smiling) Paredón.*
BOSQUES: *(In a calm, conciliatory manner)* I repeat, Mr. Castro: Mexico has granted you political asylum. I will personally escort you to the airport where two officials from my embassy are waiting for us. The three of you will then board the Mexicana Airlines flight *(looking at his watch)* departing in three hours for Mexico.
FIDEL: Three hours? But my son?
GUARD: *(Mockingly)* You should have thought of your family before you plotted to overthrow Batista.
FIDEL: *(Angrily, in a loud voice)* Cuba is my family.
BOSQUES: *(Moving to both men)* Caballeros! Gentlemen!
FIDEL: Three hours?
GUARD: *(Mocking) Paredón.*
BOSQUES: *(Addressing* CASTRO*)* Upon arriving in Mexico, you will be free and unencumbered, with the only restriction being that you will not be able to return to Cuba without the consent of the Cuban government. Your ex-wife and son—and anyone else, for that matter—will be allowed to travel to Mexico and visit you.
GUARD: *(Opening the prison door. He picks up the small suitcase)* Here. *(He hands* CASTRO *the suitcase)* A change of clothes. *(Mocking, pointing to* CASTRO'S *outfit)* You can't arrive in exile dressed like a prisoner.
FIDEL: *(Opening the suitcase)* What of my brother? And my other men?

BOSQUES: They have also been granted political asylum, Mr. Castro.
GUARD: *(Sarcastically)* Mexico's President thinks his country is big enough to hold all of Cuba's political trash.
FIDEL: *(Quietly, resigned)* Mexico?
GUARD: It's going to be a family reunion in Mexico for the Castro brothers and their group of pathetic rebels. *(Looking at* BOSQUES*)* Poor Mexico!
BOSQUES: *(Opening the folder he is carrying, taking out documents)* Here are your identity papers and travel documents, Mr. Castro. *(He hands* CASTRO *the documents;* CASTRO *scrutinizes them)* Or should I say Mr. González.
FIDEL: González? *(Examining the papers)* Alejandro González?
BOSQUES: Alejandro is your middle name, isn't it?
FIDEL: Yes. *(Pause)* But González?
BOSQUES: González in Cuba is like Chávez in Mexico or Smith in the United States.
FIDEL: What?
BOSQUES: Very common surnames.
GUARD: You'll blend in—and disappear—in masses of the Mexicans. *(Pause)* Never to reappear in Cuba again!
FIDEL: *(Softly)* Alejandro González.
GUARD: Now, get dressed! *(The guard and* BOSQUES *move back; the* GUARD *slams the prison door shut)* You have a flight to catch!
FIDEL: Mexico?
The GUARD *and* BOSQUES *walk to the door.* BOSQUES *exits. The* GUARD: *looks back at* CASTRO.
GUARD: *(Firmly)* You have five minutes to get changed. *(Pause)* A one-way ticket to Mexico City. *(Pause, sarcastically)* A free trip to Mexico! I'd like a free trip to Mexico! As I said, you are one lucky man! *(Pause, mockingly as he shuts the door with force)* Adios, Alejandro.

4

Scene 2

Mérida, Mexico. 1955

A living room in a mid-century modern house in the Santiago neighborhood of Mérida, the largest city on the Yucatán peninsula. It is the middle-class home of the Cámara family. The house boasts the modern conveniences, including a late-model black-and-white television, a telephone, and framed photographs of family members on the walls. LÍA CÁMARA, *a school teacher in a rural town, is preparing for the following week's class. Her father,* PEDRO CÁMARA, *and her mother,* SOCORRO BLUM DE CÁMARA, *are with her.*

PEDRO: *(Amused)* Always running late, with your lesson plans.
SOCORRO: Don't start, Pedro.
PEDRO: Start what?
LÍA: I can take it, Mother.
SOCORRO: The point is that you don't have to take it.
PEDRO: What's there to take?
SOCORRO: Your cynicism.
PEDRO: Me, a cynic?
LÍA: Yes, Father.
SOCORRO: And a misanthrope.
PEDRO: Oh, Lord, what have I done to be blessed with two wicked women in my life?
LÍA: Three, if you count my sister.
PEDRO: How could I forget?
SOCORRO: You forget only what's good for you.
PEDRO: *(Turning serious, to* LÍA*)* Good for me? How about good for *her*?
SOCORRO: Don't start!
PEDRO: I'm not starting, just continuing!
SOCORRO: Pedro!
PEDRO: Is teaching poor peasants in the middle of nowhere

good for you, Lía?
SOCORRO: *(Adamant)* She's a teacher, Pedro. And it just so happens that she's doing her social service in a rural community. It's both her duty and an honor.
PEDRO: *(Firmly)* Duty, yes. But an honor? Forgive me, but spending five days a week in a backwater place where people walk around barefoot ...
LÍA: It's our social responsibility to reach out to the least privileged and help them, Father. I'm a teacher so the Maya villagers can improve their lives.
PEDRO: Improve their lives?
LÍA: Yes, Father!
PEDRO: I doubt that!
SOCORRO: Why do you say that, Pedro?
PEDRO: Didn't that bishop, Diego de Landa, start schools for the Maya four centuries ago?
LÍA: And?
PEDRO: Not much progress on that front!
SOCORRO: Pedro!
PEDRO: I'm just saying. *(Pause, to* LÍA*)* Do they even speak Spanish?
LÍA: Yes, Father, they do.
PEDRO: *(Removing his reading glasses)* Really?
LÍA: *(Shyly)* For the most part.
PEDRO: Aha! They don't!
LÍA: But they're learning!
SOCORRO: Stop it, Pedro. You're mocking her!
PEDRO: I'm not mocking anyone, Socorro. It's just that the world is full of good intentions gone awry. And the result of things going awry becomes the world's misfortune.
LÍA: Father, the Maya are good people. And it makes me so happy to teach them. Besides, the new federal guidelines on school lessons for indigenous people are really working.
PEDRO: To my way of thinking, it's perfectly fair for society to ask for a return on its investment. *(Pause)* Is there?
LÍA: Is there what?

SOCORRO: Pedro, don't go there.

PEDRO: I have every right to go there. As a taxpayer.

SOCORRO: *(Imitating him)* "I have every right to go there. As a taxpayer."

PEDRO: Socorro!

LÍA: *(Laughter, as she gathers her papers)* Yes, Father, we are all better off when everyone can read and write. Even in small villages.

PEDRO: That's a lovely thought, but that's the same lovely thought we've been telling ourselves ever since—

LÍA:—the end of the Second World War.

PEDRO:—Don't interrupt me!

SOCORRO: Don't interrupt her!

The women laugh. Suddenly, offstage we hear Mozart's "Ronda Alla Turca," which continues throughout the rest of the scene.

PEDRO: *(Raising his finger, looking up)* Listen!

SOCORRO: Listen to what?

PEDRO: Ah, it's three o'clock sharp!

LÍA: *(Looking up)* It's that late?

PEDRO: She practices for three hours, your sister, every day, starting at three o'clock. *She's* going somewhere.

LÍA: Going somewhere! *(Looking up at the clock)* The bus!

PEDRO: Why can't you also be a concert pianist like your sister? That's a profession that brings beauty to the world—and is one you can pursue here, in civilization, and not—

LÍA: *(Gathering her papers and notebooks)* Not what?

PEDRO: Not stuck in a rural town.

SOCORRO: *(Sternly)* Pedro!

LÍA: *(Looking up)* That rural town is where I belong.

PEDRO: A rural town filled with . . .

LÍA: Filled with what?

PEDRO: I won't say it.

SOCORRO: Filled with what, Pedro?

LÍA: *(Approaching her father)* Say it.

PEDRO: Alright, I'm not ashamed of my thoughts: Maya peasants.

LÍA: Education will help the Maya stop being peasants and—
PEDRO:—become what?
LÍA: Modern citizens of a modern Mexico! I teach to end their alienation so they can know the world! *(To* SOCORRO*)* We continue to be a revolutionary people, isn't that right, Mother?
SOCORRO: That's what we like to think!
PEDRO: Just because the technocrats in Mexico City say such things, doesn't mean political conceits are realities.
SOCORRO: Don't be such a cynic!
PEDRO: Socorro, we stopped being a "revolutionary" anything back in the 1940s! Now we're just an ordinary country run by ordinary—meaning *self-serving*—politicians!
SOCORRO: *(To* PEDRO*)* Enough! I will not have such cynical talk while Mozart fills our home! *(To* LÍA*)* You have a bus to catch! If you miss the 3:30 bus, the next one won't get you in until nightfall.
PEDRO: Lía, honey, is it really worth a four-hour bus ride across the peninsula to teach barefoot peasants?
LÍA: *(Moving to kiss her father, then her mother, and she picks up a small suitcase before rushing for the door)* I know! I'm late! We can continue our argument—
PEDRO:—our discussions—
LÍA:—when I'm back next weekend.
SOCORRO: *(To* LÍA*)* Go! You're late as it is!
LÍA *exits. Pedro and Socorro move to each other.*
PEDRO: I worry for her.
SOCORRO: So do I.
PEDRO: I worry for her safety, the long bus rides every week—and being out there, in a forsaken town with nothing but Maya peasants—
SOCORRO:—and smelly goats.
PEDRO: Smelly goats—and smellier villagers!
SOCORRO: Don't say that!
PEDRO: Alright!
SOCORRO: But I do worry for her future. Her sister, here, has suitors. But Lía? Out there? How is she ever going

to find a suitable young man?
PEDRO: Still, she loves what she does.
SOCORRO: That, she does. *(Pause)* For now, maybe that's enough.

Mozart's music fades as the scene darkens.

Scene 3

Mexico City. 1955

A small apartment in Mexico City. FIDEL CASTRO *is smoking a cigarette, seated at a writing desk. His brother,* RAÚL CASTRO, *is pacing the room. It is sparsely furnished. There are two large maps on the wall. One is of Cuba and the other is of Mexico. There are beer bottles, bottles of rum, stacks of paper, and books about. Clothes are strewn all over the place.* FIDEL CASTRO *is reading. There is a cup of coffee next to him.* RAÚL CASTRO *is studying the map of Mexico.*

FIDEL: *(Looking up)* Are they watching?
RAÚL: *(Moving to the window, moving the curtain with discretion)* They who? Batista's spies? Mexican intelligence? The CIA?
FIDEL: Any or all. *(Standing up)* I can't stand living like this. It never stops, this constant surveillance.
RAÚL: *(Walking back to the map)* It makes no difference. Let them stare at our window all they want.
FIDEL: *(Pacing)* We're wasting our time just sitting here. We are men of action—
RAÚL: —and men of action cannot sit still.
FIDEL: That's right, Raúl. All great men who change history are men of action—not exiles wasting their time!
RAÚL: *(Firmly, turning to his brother)* No, Fidel, we are not wasting our time. We are biding our time. *(Pause)* Let the spies become bored day after day as they see us going about doing nothing. We have time.
FIDEL: We don't have time. There's momentum on our side right now, and we're losing it the longer we stay here.
RAÚL: *(Walking back to the map of Mexico, and points to it)* See? The Yucatán peninsula might be the ideal spot. But from which port? Cozumel? Playa del Carmen? Progreso?
FIDEL: We'll never find out, just sitting here in Mexico City.

10

We have to leave this place, since nothing will come from staying in this . . . *(with disdain)* Aztec capital.

RAÚL: *(Moving to the window, moving the curtain with discretion)* Fidel, you have to learn to be patient. *(Pause)* We have to put on a good show for our friends.

FIDEL: A show?

RAÚL: *(Looking at FIDEL)* Misdirection. Misinformation. Deception. *(Pause)* Let them report back nonsense. Let them believe our propaganda. The better for us to succeed.

The door bursts open and ERNESTO "CHE" GUEVARA *bounds in, with enthusiasm and exuberance, lighting up the room.*

CHE: Did you see how many fans we have? *(To FIDEL)* I think I spotted the spies from the CIA! They're on the fourth floor, the third window from the corner. Gringo bastards. We should put on a great show for them.

FIDEL: Why do you both think this is a show?

RAÚL: *(Ignoring FIDEL, to CHE)* It's going to be more than a show; it's going to be a spectacle that will change the course of history!

CHE: Exactly! *(Reaching for a bottle of rum and pouring shots for the men, then reaching for a cigar)* Intelligence services from three countries are spying on us—that means that we are of men of consequence. *(Handing the brothers shots of rum)* They're afraid of what we are capable! It's *great* to be feared! That's *power!*

FIDEL: The scrutiny, though. It's maddening.

RAÚL *and* CHE *drink their shots of rum;* FIDEL *puts his down.*

RAÚL: *(To FIDEL)* Patience, Fidel, patience. *(To CHE)* Where were you? You're more—

CHE:—alive!

FIDEL: Alive?

CHE: I'm more alive now than I was this morning!

FIDEL: What?

CHE: *(Bouncing with enthusiasm)* I can't help it, Fidel. I find this city exhilarating!

FIDEL: Exhilarating?

RAÚL: Let the boy speak.

CHE: Yes, let me get it off my chest! *(Reaching for the bottle of rum, pouring more shots for* RAÚL *and himself)* This is a country that is alive with the authenticity of revolution.

FIDEL: *(Lighting a cigarette, skeptical)* Whatever that means.

CHE: *(Moving with exuberance, while* RAÚL *looks on with admiration)* Look at Mexico! Look at at the artists, the intellectuals. They are at the center of a great debate! A *debate* about their *nation*—their *destiny*. The entire elite is engaged in lifting the peasants out of their ignorance and incorporating them in the body politic! Not like in—

RAÚL:—Cuba, Fidel.

CHE:—where blacks and mulattos remain impoverished— with no hope—

RAÚL:—and jailed when they speak out against social injustice.

CHE: But not here! *(Handing* FIDEL *and* RAÚL *shot glasses)* Why, I just came back from the public ministries. These government buildings are decorated in vast, sweeping murals! Clemente Orozco, who mocked the vanities of the bourgeoisie, has painted a hammer and sickle over the door to the national Preparatoria school! Can you imagine that over the entrance to the Universidad de La Habana? And Diego Rivera has portrayed the unstoppable swelling of life—peasants looking to the future, all races holding hands—right on the walls of the Education Ministry!

RAÚL: *(Laughing)* Calm down, calm down.

CHE: But I can't!

FIDEL: *(Moving the curtains)* When I look out the window I see old Indian women walking down the streets balancing baskets of fruit on their heads. This is the Mexico I see, a backward nation where the indigenous peoples are oppressed—and silenced.

CHE: *(Walking to* FIDEL, *moving his hand from the curtain, which falls back)* Then you are not looking at Mexico through generous eyes.

RAÚL: That's right, Fidel. *(Pause)* Has it occurred to you Mexico gave us asylum because Mexico secretly wants us to succeed?

CHE: If Mexico didn't believe in our cause, they would have you both languish in Batista's jail.

RAÚL: Asylum was Mexico's way of supporting us.

FIDEL: *(Moving the curtains once more)* This is a country that oppresses its own.

CHE: *(Moving back to the writing desk)* You're wrong, Fidel.

RAÚL: This country hates Batista as much as we do.

CHE: And, remember, this is the land of José Vasconcelos. The man who revolutionized public education. This is the country of Felipe Carrillo Puerto, who wanted to create a Communistic society for the indigenous people in the Yucatán.

RAÚL: I've heard of Felipe.

CHE: *(Turning to* RAÚL*)* And this is the *city* of *revolutionary* thinking! In Buenos Aires! In Havana! In capitalist capitals of Latin America women look to Paris for fashion, like the bourgeois scum that they are. But here? They look to the traditional clothes of the indigenous people! Don't you see? This is a country where a Mexican Jew dressed up in the indigenous clothing of the oppressed—and became the toast of the town!

RAÚL: *(Somberly)* Frida. *(Pause)* How is Diego doing?

FIDEL: Have you seen him?

CHE: I had coffee with Diego yesterday.

RAÚL: How is he holding up?

CHE: *(Turning to* RAÚL*)* Considering it's been only a year since her death, he's doing as well as can be expected. Sometimes a man never gets over a lost love. Sometimes a man never recovers from a broken heart. But not Diego. He's a strong man.

RAÚL *and* CHE *drink their shots of rum;* CHE *pours the men more.* FIDEL *continues to abstain.*

RAÚL: Poor Frida. *(Raising his shot glass)* A toast!

RAÚL *and* CHE *drink their shots of rum.*

FIDEL: And you ask me to be patient, Raúl? Don't you see how quickly anyone can just die in a moment? There's Frida, at a Communist rally one day, and a month later, she's dead from pneumonia.

CHE: *(Turning to* FIDEL*)* That's why we must absorb as much as we can from Mexico! The revolution here has been more successful than the revolution in Russia.

FIDEL: How?

CHE: The Revolution here has been embraced, not resisted.

RAÚL: He's right. *(Turning to* FIDEL*)* Russia's revolution forced millions of Russians into exile, creating a Russian Diaspora in Europe. That didn't happen here.

CHE: *(Turning to* FIDEL*)* Here, the *elite* champion revolution.

FIDEL: *(Turning to* CHE*)* Then why are we under constant surveillance?

CHE: *(Moving to the window, drawing the curtain wide open, and he jumps on a small table)* Who cares? Who cares who's spying on us? *(Turning his back to the window, undoing his belt, and bendimg over)* They can watch all they want!

CHE *moons out the window, jumps off the table, and adjusts his pants.*

FIDEL: *(Angry)* Che!

RAÚL: *(Walking to* CHE*)* You are something enthralling, my boy!

CHE: I repeat: Mexico is the land of authentic revolution!

RAÚL: *(Kissing* CHE *atop his head)* Then you must become the Apostle of our Revolution!

CHE: *(Rushing for the door)* I intend to be!

FIDEL: Where are you off to?

CHE: David Siqueiros is having a salon at his painting studio. He invites Communist poets to inspire his art for the masses, then he shares the plunder from selling his works of art to the bourgeoisie with them! It's beautiful!

RAÚL: Plunder? *(Pause)* Ah, drink and food for Communist poets! Courtesy of capitalist fools!

CHE: The Americans, they can scheme and plot all they want, but they will never crush the revolutionary zeal of Mexico. This is what authenticity means!

RAÚL: Like Marx said: Greedy capitalists will sell us the rope we will use to hang them!

RAÚL *watches with admiration as* CHE *bounds out, closing the door. Fidel draws the curtains close.*

Raúl: Such a beautiful boy! I like him so much.

FIDEL: I know you do. *(Pause)* But you can't like him *that* way, Raúl.

The men stare at each other.

RAÚL: *(Walking to the maps on the wall)* You have to go to the Yucatán. That's where we'll leave Mexico for Cuba. I'm sure of it.

FIDEL: Hernán Cortés set sail from Havana to Mexico—

RAÚL:—So it's only poetic that we sail from Mexico to conquer Havana!

FIDEL: Tonight, then. I'll sneak out and go to the bus station.

RAÚL: You know it's a thirty-hour bus ride, don't you?

FIDEL: If it were a thirty-day bus ride, I wouldn't complain. Anything to get out of Mexico City.

Scene 4

Valladolid, Mexico. 1955

LÍA CÁMARA *is sitting on a bus. She is holding a book in her hands. We hear the murmur of voices indicating a crowd of passengers. There are boxes and small suitcases in the overhead bins. The passengers can be silhouettes or images projected. The bus driver's voice announces, "Departing for Mérida, last call."* FIDEL CASTRO *enters the bus. There is only one empty seat, the aisle seat next to her.*

FIDEL: Is this seat available?
LÍA: *(Smiling)* It won't be if you sit down.
FIDEL: *(In a charming manner, removing his hat with a flourish)* Then I will.
We hear the sound of the closing door and the bus pulling out of the station. We hear the bus driver say "Next stop, Mérida." LÍA *returns to her book.*
FIDEL: *(Interrupting her)* How long is the bus ride from here?
LÍA: *(Looking up)* From Valladolid?
FIDEL: Yes.
LÍA: Three hours.
FIDEL: I had hoped it wouldn't be that long.
She returns to her book. He fidgets with a map. After a moment he interrupts her again.
FIDEL: Does the Port of Progreso have a marina?
LÍA: *(Smiling, putting her book down, after an awkward pause)* You're not from here, are you?
FIDEL: No, I'm not.
LÍA: Do you know how I knew that?
FIDEL: *(Intrigued)* No, tell me.
LÍA: *(Flirting)* Gentlemen around here are in the custom of introducing themselves when they encounter a charming young woman. And they seldom interrupt a young lady who's reading a book.

FIDEL: Is that so?

LÍA: Yes, that's so.

FIDEL: Then I'll keep that in mind when I encounter a charming young woman reading a book.

They both laugh.

LÍA: *(She closes the book and places it on her lap)* I am Lía Cámara. And you are?

FIDEL: I am—*(Pause)*—Alejandro, Alejandro González.

LÍA: Well, I am delighted to meet you, Alejandro.

FIDEL: It's a pleasure, Ms. Cámara.

LÍA: Don't think using an honorific will excuse your lack of manners.

FIDEL: Lack of manners? That stings!

They laugh.

LÍA: *(Returning to her book)* Yes, it does.

Fidel: Yes, what does?

LÍA: *(Looking up)* A marina. *(Pause)* Didn't you ask if the Port of Progreso had a marina?

FIDEL: Oh, yes, yes I did.

LÍA *looks away, returning to her book.* FIDEL *scribbles notes on his map, which occupies him. They continue in this way for a short time before he interrupts her again.*

FIDEL: What are you reading?

LÍA: *(Somewhat annoyed, putting the book down)* Well, I'm trying to read a novel.

FIDEL: You are?

LÍA: Yes, I am.

FIDEL: What is it?

LÍA: *Lolita.*

FIDEL: Nabokov?

LÍA: Yes, Vladimir Nabokov. It was a sensation last year, best seller in Europe and the U.S. This is the first Spanish-language translation.

FIDEL: It's a good story, I've been told.

LÍA: Well, when I'm able to read it without interruption, I'll let you know what I think.

LÍA *returns to her book.* FIDEL *busies himself with his map. After a moment, he speaks up.*

FIDEL: Do you find Lolita a corrupt child? Or is the novel the anguished story of a bourgeois man of taste and education who can love only little girls?

LÍA: *(Closing the book and putting it away)* Perhaps I'll just wait for the film to come out, since it seems you're determined to keep me from reading it.

FIDEL: *(Embarrassed)* Oh, I apologize, Ms. Cámara, but you look so attractive when you're reading—

LÍA:—that you can't help but interrupt me!

FIDEL: No, not at all! *(Pause)* Well, yes, you're right.

FIDEL *awkwardly returns to his map.* LÍA *stares at him. After a moment, it is she who interrupts him.*

LÍA: And what brought Alejandro to the rural town of Valladolid? It's not often you see men like yourself riding a bus back to Mérida.

FIDEL: It isn't?

LÍA: Look around us!

He looks around, noticing that most of the passengers are Maya people.

FIDEL: I see what you mean—

LÍA: All Maya!

FIDEL: Why is that?

LÍA: Privileged people have cars these days; they drive themselves wherever they want. Bus transportation is for—

FIDEL:—the masses?

LÍA: I was going to say, for the public.

FIDEL: Public transportation is mass transportation, isn't it?

LÍA: You sound like my father!

FIDEL: *(Surprised)* Your father?

LÍA: Yes. *(Pause)* He loves polemics.

FIDEL: You were right.

LÍA: About what?

FIDEL: About being charming.

LÍA: *(Embarrassed)* You do know I was joking.

FIDEL: Is that what you are? A charming Mexican joker?

LÍA: Alejandro is mistaken on both accounts.

FIDEL: Oh?

LÍA: I am Yucatecan, not Mexican. And I am a teacher, not a joker.

FIDEL: A Yucatecan? Isn't the Yucatán part of Mexico?

LÍA: If you want to get technical, then, yes, the Yucatán is part of Mexico. But the Yucatán is not Mexico.

FIDEL: And I thought you said I was the one who was into polemics!

They laugh.

LÍA: You do know this three-hour bus ride will seem like an eternity.

FIDEL: Or not.

LÍA: Who's the charmer now?

FIDEL: *(Pointing to her, jokingly)* And what does this charmer do?

LÍA: I suppose I charm my students, or at least try. I'm a teacher.

FIDEL: A teacher.

LÍA: Yes. A teacher.

FIDEL: Well, then it's my lucky day.

LÍA: Why do you say that?

FIDEL: Because I'm a student.

LÍA; A student?

She laughs.

FIDEL: Is that funny? You don't think I'm capable of learning?

LÍA: I'm not sure I can teach you anything, from the looks of you!

FIDEL: Try.

LÍA: Try what?

FIDEL: Try to teach me.

LÍA: Teach you what?

FIDEL: Anything.

LÍA: Something tells me the only thing I could teach you is the Golden Rule.

FIDEL: Really?

LÍA: Something also tells me that that's probably the only thing you don't know—but you also have no interest in learning.

FIDEL: Now, I'm the one who's intrigued!
LÍA: Intrigued about what?
FIDEL: Well, I find a teacher who doesn't think she can teach a student the Golden Rule is an intriguing teacher.
LÍA: Intriguing? *(Pause)* I thought I was charming!
FIDEL: Who says a beautiful woman can't be both charming and intriguing.
LÍA: Oh, I like this Alejandro!
FIDEL: And I like this Mexican—I mean, Yucatecan—teacher sitting next to me on this bus!
LÍA: A student, you said.
FIDEL: Yes, a student. That's all I am.
LÍA: And what is Alejandro a student of?
FIDEL: History.
LÍA: *(Laughing)* History?
FIDEL: Is that funny?
LÍA: No, not at all. That's impressive, if I say so.
FIDEL: I'm glad that the Maestra Lía approves.
LÍA: That will depend.
FIDEL: Depend on what?
LÍA: The kind of history you study.
FIDEL: What if I told you I am a student of Mexican history?
LÍA: I find that peculiar—considering you're Cuban.
FIDEL: Cuban? How did you know?
LÍA: Your accent for one. Your accent for second. Your accent for third.

They laugh.

FIDEL: It's that obvious?
LÍA: A Cuban student of Mexican history. Now I'm the one who's intrigued!
FIDEL: I know all about the great men of the Mexican Revolution—Emiliano Zapata, Francisco Madero, Pancho Villa. These are the men of action who forged modern Mexico.
LÍA: Very good! *(Pause)* And, may I ask, what takes you to Mérida?
FIDEL: The airport, to catch a flight. *(Pause)* I've spent quite

some time here in Yucatán, and now I'm headed back to Mexico City.
LÍA: What's in Mexico City?
FIDEL: My brother.
LÍA: I see.
FIDEL: And some . . . friends.
LÍA: Are they also students of Mexican history?
FIDEL: You could say that.
LÍA: Tell me, what are you going to do in Mexico City?
FIDEL: I'm anxious to see the great murals that celebrate the Mexican Revolution.
LÍA: I'm impressed.
FIDEL: You are?
LÍA: Not too many Cubans fly to Mexico City to see the murals commemorating our Revolution.
FIDEL: This one does. *(Pause)* Are you familiar with Cuban revolutionaries?
LÍA: Of course I am. As a student of Mexican history, you should know that your José Martí spent considerable time in Mérida when he lived in Mexico.
FIDEL: And he spoke fondly of Mexico—her people, her hospitality, and her generosity of spirit for Latin American liberators.
LÍA: We try to be true to our Revolution!
FIDEL: I know. *(Pause)* I don't think there's a Cuban alive who doesn't know how Mexico offered José Martí sanctuary when he needed it.
LÍA: True.
FIDEL: And every Cuban aspires to make José Martí proud.
LÍA: It sounds to me that you're well versed in history—Mexico's and Cuba's. What can I possibly teach you?
FIDEL: Apart from the Golden Rule?
They laugh.
LÍA: I will be happy to teach you anything I can.
FIDEL: Very well, then. *(Pause)* Here's something I've been pondering.
LÍA: Ask away, Alejandro.
FIDEL: How has Mexico managed to pursue its own

independent course when it shares a border with that imperialistic neighbor to its north?

LÍA: *(Laughing)* Imperialist?

FIDEL: Yes! They're overbearing, the Americans!

LÍA: "El Monstruo," José Martí called the United States.

FIDEL: *Viví en el monstruo y le conozco las entrañas.*

LÍA: The complete phrase is, "I have lived in the monster and I know its entrails; my sling is David's."

FIDEL: *(Impressed)* This Yucatecan teacher sitting by my side is fine a student of Cuban history, I see!

LÍA: *(Showing off, to impress him)* José Martí wrote that in his last letter to Manuel Mercado in the spring of 1895. The letter remains unfinished; the Cuban leader died on the battlefield the next day.

They stare at each other. He brushes up against her arm momentarily; she is startled at first, then looks down.

FIDEL: *(In a tender manner)* Something tells me you can teach me more than the Golden Rule. Something tells me you can teach me much about history—and life.

LÍA: I'm not sure about that. But what I can teach you is that three things make it possible for Mexico to get along with the United States.

FIDEL: And what are they?

LÍA *hesitates. The following exchange is one of flirtation.*

LÍA: *(With reluctance)* No, it's complicated.

FIDEL: I like complications. Try me.

LÍA: No, it'll make me sound like a history nerd.

FIDEL: *(Jokingly)* Are you a nerd?

LÍA: Well, I can name the capital of every state. Does that make me a nerd?

FIDEL: I suppose it does.

LÍA: There you have it! I'm a nerd!

FIDEL: What makes you think *I'm* not a nerd? *(Pointing to his face)* I'm wearing glasses. And I studied law.

LÍA: Eyeglasses! Law books!

FIDEL: A nerd, like I said.

LÍA: Well, if you're game.

FIDEL: And game I am—I might even fall for a charming

Mexican Maestra who can offer insights on our neighbor to the north—"El Monstruo!"

LÍA: Very well, then, Alejandro.

FIDEL: I'm all ears, Maestra!

LÍA: *(Self-consciously at first, but with growing confidence)* First, there is language. It takes effort to speak to each other, so we just smile politely and ignore each other as much as we can. *(*FIDEL *laughs)* The second is a vast desert along the border: Most Americans live north of the border desert and most Mexicans live south of the border desert. *(*FIDEL *laughs again)* And the third is a natural, mutual repulsion we have for the other. *(*LÍA *clears her throat)* I mean, we are warm Catholics and they are cold Protestants. We, Catholics, include and they, Protestants, exclude. Fortunately, we don't want to include them and they're happing excluding us, so it all works out for the best in the end. *(Pause)* We are, in fact, like oil and water.

FIDEL: If that's the secret to your country's success, then what's to be of Cuba?

LÍA: What do you mean?

FIDEL: We only have ninety miles of water to protect us from the tentacles of that Empire, not hundreds of miles of desert.

LÍA: A body of water is not as effective as a desert wasteland, do you think?

FIDEL: It's not: the Straits of Florida offer no defense.

LÍA: I see. *(Pause)* Then that explains why the tentacles of America's Mafia have a firm grip on Cuba—or at least its casinos and—

FIDEL:—and what?

LÍA: Well, I don't want to say it.

FIDEL: Say it, say it! I want to hear what Mexicans think of the American presence in Cuba!

LÍA: *(After an awkward pause)* Its houses of ill repute.

FIDEL: *(Laughing)* You mean the Mafia's whorehouses!

LÍA: I didn't want to say it.

FIDEL: You know what they also say?

LÍA: What?

FIDEL: That in the United States, you can be anything you want to be.

LÍA: I've heard that too.

FIDEL: Too bad so many Americans want to be assholes.

LÍA: *(With one hand rising to her mouth and the other squeezing* FIDEL'S *thigh)* Alejandro! Such language!

FIDEL: *(Laughing at his mischief)* If the noun fits—use it!

LÍA: You Cubans have a reputation for being foul-mouthed for good reason!

FIDEL: If the situation calls for it!

LÍA: No! No! No!

FIDEL: *(Touching her hand)* Your hand?

LÍA: *(Recoiling in embarrassment)* I'm so sorry!

FIDEL: *(Smiling)* I'm not!

LÍA: *(In a stern manner, clearing her throat and regaining her composure)* I'm not making another commentary on Cuba.

FIDEL: *(Raising is hand to his heart in a dramatic fashion)* Oh, *Maestra* Lía! Whorehouses! The word is like a knife in this patriot's heart! *(Feigning shock)* Corruption in Cuba under Bastista? Never! *(Raising his eyebrows)* The Mafia in Cuba under Batista? Never! *(Making a sign of the cross)* Whorehouses in Cuba under Batista? Never! *(Shaking his head)* Is that what charming and intriguing teachers in Mexico think of Cuba?

She laughs, leaning into his direction.

LÍA: No comment! *(Pause)* But to answer your question about our relationship with the United States, it was the mutual respect and understanding between two presidents—Franklin Roosevelt and Lázaro Cárdenas—that set the precedent that each country would evolve and find its own way. And each respects the other.

FIDEL: Evolve? Find its own way? *(Earnestly)* Teach my inner nerd!

LÍA: Very well: since the end of the Second World War, Mexican history is the struggle to implement the principles of our Revolution.

FIDEL: In a word, pragmatism.

LÍA: *(Correcting him gently)* In a phrase, scientific determinism.

FIDEL: And what does that mean?

LÍA: *(Pause)* Well, I think it means that, as a society, our government, in good faith, is trying to reconcile the competing demands of our ancient traditions and our modern aspirations.

FIDEL: This student needs a lesson!

They laugh.

LÍA: Let me see if I can explain myself. *(Pause)* I'm a teacher in a town called Tizimín. Most of the inhabitants are Maya. This indigenous nation is at the margin of society. I teach them in the hope that once they can read and write they will improve their lives. I teach them with the expectation that they will be able to enjoy the material benefits of the modern world.

FIDEL: How does it work? This teaching? Do you teach children? Adults? Both?

LÍA: I teach primarily children, but some adults.

FIDEL: Is there a difference in how you teach each group of students?

LÍA: Of course there is!

FIDEL: Really?

LÍA: In my case, there are challenges specific to the reality of rural Yucatán.

FIDEL: Meaning what?

LÍA: Most adults are proficient in Spanish, but cannot read or write it.

FIDEL: Proficient in Spanish?

LÍA: You don't know?

FIDEL: Know what?

LÍA: Most of the people in the Yucatán speak Maya.

FIDEL: Maya? That language survives?

LÍA: *(Laughing)* Survives? It *thrives!* In fact, the indigenous language of Yucatec Maya is the most-widely spoken indigenous language in North America!

FIDEL: In North America?

LÍA: Yes!

FIDEL: It thrives?

LÍA: More than a million people speak Yucatec Maya, Alejandro. *(Pause)* So the challenge for me is the fact that children speak Yucatec Maya at home, and they have to learn to speak Spanish in school. For the adults, on the other hand, they speak Spanish to get by in the world, but they can't speak or write it.

FIDEL: This sounds complicated.

LÍA: It is, which is why there are decades of experience in how to teach each group of students, adult or children.

FIDEL: In Cuba, our peasants are illiterate. We call them *guajiros*, country folk. The dictator Batista refuses to build schools, since knowledge is power and the last thing he wants is an educated and empowered citizenry.

LÍA: We could set up a program *(snapping her fingers)*, just like that!

FIDEL: You could?

LÍA: An adult literacy program, of course. *(Pause)* If Cuban *guajiros* speak Spanish, then teaching to read and write is simple.

FIDEL: I'm glad I took this seat.

LÍA: And so am I!

They laugh.

FIDEL: And, apart from education, what promises remain to be kept?

LÍA: Promises? The Revolution's promises?

FIDEL: Yes, I'd like to understand how modern Mexico is going about fulfilling the ideals of its Revolution.

LÍA: Well, the brief answer is that we are working to reconcile the conflicts between private wants and public needs. This means that there are certain things we want as a society for all—schools, healthcare, civil tranquility—but we also respect the right of the individual to pursue private dreams. It's about reconciliation to achieve the superior societal outcome.

FIDEL: *(Intrigued, slowly)* A superior societal outcome. *(Pause)* And how are you going about that? That reconciliation?

LÍA: To a large extent, we look to the indigenous people.

FIDEL: What does that mean?

LÍA: Well, where I teach, the Maya hold land communally—

FIDEL: —communally?

LÍA: Well, the villagers get together and decide who can work which plot, and how to share the burdens that benefit all the people who live in that village.

FIDEL: It sounds like communism to me.

LÍA: No, it's not communism; it's *communalism*. There's a difference.

FIDEL: Is there?

LÍA: Of course there is! Communalism is a form of economic organization. But communism is a political ideology.

FIDEL: What a smart teacher you are! You remind me of that other book on the best seller list these days!

LÍA: Oh? Which one?

FIDEL: *The Affluent Society*.

LÍA: Haven't heard of it.

FIDEL: It's by a Canadian economist, John Kenneth Galbraith.

LÍA: Have you read it?

FIDEL: Most of it. *(Pause)* He's concerned with social issues—and communalism.

LÍA: Canada also struggles over their indigenous peoples.

FIDEL: I think every country does.

LÍA: We had a governor here, Felipe Carrillo Puerto, who championed the communalistic aspirations of the Maya people. But many people—many of the rich, powerful, and privileged people—assumed he was a Communist.

FIDEL: And what happened?

LÍA: He was arrested and executed by a firing squad back in 1924. Today, he's remembered as the Apostle of the Bronze Race, meaning the Maya.

FIDEL: Just like José Martí is the Apostle of Cuban independence.

LÍA: It's possible to kill a man, but not his ideas. There are schools named after him.

FIDEL: Meaning?
LÍA: That having a school named in your honor is the greatest achievement one can realize in life, more than having a statue of gold raised in your honor.
FIDEL: Is that so?
LÍA: Yes, Alejandro, that's so.
FIDEL: Where does that leave the Mexican Revolution today?
LÍA: Where it belongs: working to reconcile the conflicts between private wants and public needs, trying to find where our traditions of communalism end and the realm of private aspirations begin.
FIDEL: Tell me more!

The scene darkens and we hear an instrumental of "Caminante del Mayab" by Guty Cárdenas, drowning out FIDEL *and* LÍA. *This suggests the passage of time. It is clear that* LÍA *and* FIDEL *are engaged in animated conversation, moving their heads and gesticulating, leaning close. After a minute, the music subsides, the lights rise, and we hear the bus driver announce, "Arriving at Mérida Central Bus Terminal." We also hear* FIDEL *and* LÍA *again.*

LÍA: We're here!
FIDEL: Already?
LÍA: Goodness, Alejandro! We've been talking for three hours.
FIDEL: That can't be!
LÍA: Well, it must be, since we've arrived.
FIDEL: I'm staying at the Reforma Hotel downtown, just three nights. Then I go back to Mexico City.
The bus stops; passengers begin to get up, gather their belongings, and disembark. FIDEL *and* LÍA *stand up. He helps get her small suitcase down.*
LÍA: That's a lovely hotel. Art Deco and comfortable.
FIDEL: I'd like to continue our conversation.
LÍA: You do know I live with my parents and my sister.
FIDEL: A good student is always respectful of his teacher.

They laugh.
LÍA: I suppose you're presentable enough to invite over!
They walk to the door, then exit the bus.
FIDEL: May I have your telephone number?
FIDEL *reaches for a matchbook in his pocket and takes a pen from his shirt pocket, handing them to her.*
LÍA: Yes, you can have my number. *(She takes the matchbook cover)* I, also, would love to continue our conversation!
She writes her telephone number on the matchbook cover.
FIDEL: Something tells me we've only begun to discuss history—and its meaning.
LÍA: History is a work in progress, remember that.
FIDEL: *(Playfully)* Is it?
LÍA: Yes, it's the narrative of human achievement, informed by how our understanding and values change over time—
FIDEL: —and how we, as individuals and a society, strive for the superior societal outcome.
LÍA: *(Laughing)* You *did* pay attention to me!
FIDEL: Superior societal outcome? *(Chuckling)* Talk about polemics!
LÍA: The greater good for all, that's what good government is all about.
FIDEL: Spoken like a true optimist!
LÍA: *(Laughing)* And history nerd!
FIDEL: I'll call you this evening after I settle in, *Maestra* Lía.
LÍA: And I'll answer the telephone when you do, *Estudiante* Alejandro.

They laugh, shake hands, and go their ways.

Scene 5

Mexico City. 1955

A small apartment in Mexico City. CHE GUEVARA *is at dissecting a dead cat on a table. It is sparsely furnished. There are two large maps on the wall. One is of Cuba and the other is of Mexico. There are beer bottles, bottles of rum, stacks of paper, and books about. Clothes are strewn all over the place.* RAÚL *enters the apartment, interrupting* CHE.

RAÚL: *(Entering the room, carrying books)* What are you doing?
CHE: *(Looking up)* I'm studying the internal abdominal oblique muscle of this cat.
RAÚL: Why?
CHE: Why not?
RAÚL: Where did you get that cat, anyway?
CHE: *(Dissecting the cat)* In the alley, a block away.
RAÚL: You found the corpse of a feral cat?
CHE: *(Looking up)* Not exactly.
RAÚL: What do you mean, not exactly?
CHE: *(Nonchalantly)* It's one of the feral cats living in the alley around the block. I caught him. And I drowned him so I could cut it open.
RAÚL: *(Taken aback)* You drowned the cat
CHE: Yeah. *(Pointing to the bathroom)* In the sink. I held his head underwater.
RAÚL: *(Quietly)* I see.
CHE: *(Picking up the cat with one hand, turning around, and holding the cat like a rag doll, or like Yorick's skull, as he speaks)* You should have seen him. *(With growing enthusiasm, he is animated)* There's a thrill in having power over life and death. I picked up the cat by the scruff—
RAÚL:—and then?
CHE: *(Moving about, as if in a dance)* And then I bid the

doomed, wretched animal farewell. I filled the sink with warm water, and I drowned the cat.

RAÚL: And you're cutting him up?

CHE: *(Shrugging his shoulders)* Why not? When I was in medical school in Buenos Aires, autopsies were my favorite activity. I could cut into and dissect a corpse all day!

RAÚL: What do you plan to do with the dead cat?

CHE: What difference does it make? *(Pause)* Toss it in the garbage. Who cares? What matters is that I am learning the discipline necessary to exact justice, revolutionary justice.

RAÚL: *(Walking to the window, moving the curtain with discretion)* Really?

CHE: A victorious Revolution will dispense with bourgeois formalities of trials and appeals and prison sentences. Any man who has a bank account is a man who has stolen from the proletariat! Any man who owns a business is a man who has stolen from society! Those with bank accounts and those with business are leeches sucking the life blood of the people! And we know what the enemies of the proletariat deserve: the *paredón*.

RAÚL: *(Smiling)* Firing squads, for revolutionary justice.

CHE: Yes! *(With pride)* And, as the Apostle of the Cuban Revolution, I decree that we need revolutionaries who are unmoved by bourgeois sentimentality. We must become lean, mean killing machines to cleanse society!

RAÚL: *(Smiling, moving to* CHE*)* I like the way you think, Che. *(He pats* CHE *on the cheek, almost caressing his face)* I like your approach, your pragmatism.

The door opens and FIDEL *enters. He stops, staring at* RAÚL'S *hand on* CHE'S *cheek.* RAÚL *is startled.*

FIDEL: Are you slapping Che for killing defenseless animals again?

CHE: The cat had claws! He could have defended himself! *(Pause)* But you know my nature well, don't you, Fidel?

FIDEL: It was a defenseless animal.

CHE: *(Laughing, holding the cat high)* No, Fidel, this is a capitalist cat that met revolutionary justice.

CHE *moves to the table and places the cat down.* RAÚL, *self-conscious, is embarrassed.* FIDEL *puts his suitcase down, removes his scarf and coat.*

RAÚL: How did it go?

FIDEL: *(Taking his gloves off)* It was a tremendous trip!

CHE: Was it?

RAÚL: Cozumel? Playa del Carmen? Isla Mujeres?

FIDEL: I have ideas, but there are other ports to consider before we make a final decision.

CHE: Progreso? Puerto Telchac?

FIDEL: Yes, as I said, there are other possibilities.

RAÚL: Are people there sympathetic to our cause?

CHE: Do they hate Batista?

RAÚL: *(Chuckling)* Do they know who Batista is?

FIDEL: *(Turning to his brother)* I met the most remarkable woman.

CHE: A woman?

FIDEL: A teacher. A rural teacher with an incredible command of history.

RAÚL: A teacher. *(Pause)* Teachers are important. When we triumph, we will decree a "Year of Education"—

CHE:—and we will assemble an army of "Literacy Brigades."

FIDEL: She's the ideal candidate to help us, when the time comes. *(Pacing slowly, enamored)* That woman is really amazing, something special.

CHE: You sound smitten, Fidel.

FIDEL: I'm impressed, that's for sure. *(Pause)* The woman has a sincere commitment to social justice, and she's so smart.

CHE: Smart?

RAÚL: By Mexican standards, or by normal standards?

CHE *and* RAÚL *laugh.*

FIDEL: Very funny. *(Turning to* RAÚL*)* She's a remarkable woman. A most remarkable woman. And attractive, too.

RAÚL: Good! We can use her!

FIDEL: *(Surprised)* Use her?

RAÚL: *(Pointing to the window)* They were aware you were

gone.
FIDEL: Who?
RAÚL: Our friends across the street.
CHE: They're not that stupid.
RAÚL: We thought we were clever, with your leaving here in the middle of the night for the bus station. But the next morning, one of the spies was missing. They knew you were gone and I suspect they were looking for you.
CHE: *(Moving to the window, drawing the curtain open)* Hey, *maricones*, he's back! *(He points to* FIDEL*)* El Comandante is back!
RAÚL: *(Drawing the curtains closed, angry)* Che! Discipline!
FIDEL: What do you mean, "use" her?
RAÚL: Did you meet her family?
FIDEL: Yes, I did. Why?
RAÚL: Good! She can be your cover.
FIDEL: Cover?
RAÚL: When you go back, take them with you to Progreso, Puerto Telchac, wherever. A man traveling with a family won't arouse suspicion.
FIDEL: A cover?
RAÚL: Fidel, a man traveling *alone* arouses suspicions. And you are a Cuban in the Yucatán, a Cuban male all by himself.
CHE: But a man with a girl and her mother, that's unexceptional.
RAÚL: She's your cover.
FIDEL: Pretend we're dating. *(Pause)* I get it.
CHE *rushes to the window, pulls the curtains open, turns around, jumps on the small table again, and moons the spies across the street.*
CHE: Get a good look of my asshole, assholes!
RAÚL: *(Angrily closing the curtain)* Che! Discipline!
CHE: What? Just a little fun.
RAÚL: Like killing the cat?
CHE: It was just a cat.
RAÚL: Discipline! *(He shakes his finger at* CHE *as he adjusts his pants)* Discipline, my boy.

FIDEL: You're right, Raúl. I have to go back.

RAÚL: And that Mexican family will give you anonymity.

FIDEL: I have to go back a week from today at dawn. I'll bus over, and fly back when it's time.

RAÚL: A Mexican teacher and her family. (Pause) *Idiotas útiles*—useful idiots, *polezniye duraki*, as Lenin said. Who can find fault with that?

Scene 6

Mérida, Mexico. 1956

The Cámara family residence. PEDRO CÁMARA *is sitting reading the newspaper. Offstage we hear Iberia by Isaac Albéniz;* LÍA CÁMARA'S *sister is practicing her piano.*

PEDRO: *(Looking up at the clock, to himself)* Where can they be?

Suddenly, the door opens. SOCORRO, LÍA, *and* FIDEL *enter. They are laughing and chatting.* SOCORRO *carries a folded beach blanket draped over her arm;* LÍA *carries a small picnic basket;* FIDEL *carries a larger picnic basket and a closed beach umbrella.*

SOCORRO: You should have come, Pedro! We had a wonderful time!
PEDRO: One chaperone is one chaperone too many, if you ask me.
LÍA: Mother is right. *(Placing the picnic basket on a table)* The beach was beautiful! We had a great time. *(Reaching into an oversize bag she carries)* Look, we even had our picture taken.
PEDRO: *(To* LÍA, *taking the photograph)* It sure looks like you all had fun. *(Laughing)* But look at that red polka dot scarf around Alejandro!
SOCORRO: That scarf's mine!
PEDRO: I know it is! But why he wearing it?
LÍA: It was windy!
SOCORRO: Besides, it's a great scarf! It's the same scarf that Grace Kelly wore in *Look* magazine.
PEDRO: Well, Alejandro's not Grace Kelly; he looks silly it.
SOCORRO: *(Sternly)* It's a great photograph, Pedro!
LÍA: *(Taking the photograph from her* PEDRO'S *hand)* Great? It's unforgettable! *(Admiring the photograph)*

Look at that smile! *(Looking at* FIDEL*)* Unforgettable!
SOCORRO: You should frame it!
LÍA: I will.
PEDRO: You know she will, Socorro. *(To* FIDEL*)* That scarf aside, I see you took good care of my wife and daughter, Alejandro.
SOCORRO: *(Pointing up)* Is that Isaac Albéniz?
PEDRO: She's playing "Iberia." Like clockwork, her practices.
SOCORRO: *(To* LÍA *and* FIDEL*)* Let me go let your sister know we're home—and listen to her practice.
LÍA: Go ahead, Mother.
SOCORRO *exits.*
PEDRO: *(Turning to* FIDEL*)* So, what did you think of Progreso, Alejandro?
FIDEL: I was impressed. Quite a pier—and a great lighthouse.
LÍA: *(Taking the umbrella from* FIDEL'S *hand)* You should have seen him, Father. You'd think he was an engineer, the way he examined the pier up and down!
FIDEL: *(To* LÍA*)* Was I that obvious? *(To* PEDRO*)* I just found it an impressive structure.
PEDRO: A century ago, the principal port was Sisal, but with today's modern engineering, it's Progreso.
SOCORRO *enters.*
SOCORRO: Would anyone like coffee? I know I would.
PEDRO: Yes, that's a great idea.
LÍA: How's—
SOCORRO:—your sister will be out when she's done practicing. *(To* PEDRO*)* Would you be kind enough to assist me?
PEDRO: Why? Do you suddenly need my help to make coffee?
SOCORRO: Because ... *(She looks at* LÍA *and* FIDEL*)* Just because ...
PEDRO: Just because you suddenly need my help to make coffee?
SOCORRO: No, Pedro! *(Moving sternly to him)* Because the

kids might want a moment alone, while I prepare coffee and you can watch me prepare coffee!

LIA *looks down and giggles;* FIDEL *is embarrassed.*

PEDRO: Okay, okay!

SOCORRO: *(To Lía)* We'll only be a short while.

PEDRO:—trust me, we'll be quite a while!

SOCORRO *ribs him with her elbow.*

SOCORRO: *(To* PEDRO*)* It wouldn't if you knew how to operate that espresso machine!

PEDRO: I'm not an engineer! Maybe Alejandro can figure it out!

FIDEL: An espresso machine?

LÍA: *(Looking first as* PEDRO*, then* FIDEL*)* It's a contraption we bought when we were in Miami last year! Supposed to be the latest and greatest—

PEDRO:—and it doesn't work right. *(To* SOCORRO*)* I told you that only the Italians can make espresso machines! *(To* LÍA*)* Americans have no history of coffee culture! They don't get it, and it will take half a century before they appreciate the nuances of coffee!

FIDEL: *(To* LÍA*)* You were in the United States?

LÍA: Yes, last year.

SOCORRO: *(With pride)* I went—and I took my two daughters!

PEDRO: *(To* FIDEL*)* Pan Am was having a special fare to Miami. And they jumped at the chance to fly off to Miami on a Pan Am tour—and abandon me!

SOCORRO: What of it? It was still a vacation, even if it was a tour package.

PEDRO: I didn't say it wasn't a vacation!

SOCORRO: You're making us sound like tightwads!

FIDEL *laughs.*

LÍA: *(To* FIDEL*)* Yes, it's true. Pan Am had a special promotion on its nonstop Mérida-Miami route. They even threw in a hotel—

SOCORRO: The San Juan hotel in Miami Beach!

LÍA: And the three of us went for sightseeing and—

SOCORRO:—shopping.

PEDRO: Burdines. *(Mocking)* "The Florida Store."

SOCORRO: It's a lovely store!

LÍA: When you live in the Yucatán—it's easier to get to Havana or Miami than it is to Mexico City.

FIDEL: It is?

PEDRO: Less than a two-hour flight to Miami, just over two hours to Mexico City. And if you want to take a bus to Mexico City—

SOCORRO:—it's thirty hours!

FIDEL: I know.

LÍA: *(Surprised)* You do?

PEDRO: So these three go to Miami and come back with—

SOCORRO:—all kinds of nice things!

FIDEL: *(To* LÍA*)* What did you think of Miami?

LÍA: *(With reluctance)* It was . . . different. Yes, it was different.

SOCORRO: *(Admonishing)* Lía, that's not entirely accurate.

PEDRO: Don't be embarrassed, Lía. Tell Alejandro what you really think.

Lía: *(Quietly)* Well, I *am* embarrassed.

SOCORRO: You should never be shy about speaking your mind, Lía.

PEDRO: *(To* FIDEL*)* My wife and daughters found Miami terrifying.

FIDEL: Terrifying?

LÍA: *(With reluctance)* Well, yes and no.

SOCORRO: Then explain yourself!

LÍA: *(More confident as she speaks)* The truth is that Miami is a beautiful city. We stayed at a lovely hotel in Miami Beach and we went shopping in downtown Miami. Biscayne Boulevard is a broad, modern thoroughfare—

SOCORRO:—it reminded me of the Malecón in Havana.

PEDRO: *(To* SOCORRO*)* Let her speak! You wanted her to speak her mind and now you're interrupting her!

SOCORRO: *(To* PEDRO*)* Oh, alright. *(To* LÍA*)* Go on, my dear.

LÍA: Yes, it's a beautiful boulevard. And we walked from that Spanish-style building—

SOCORRO: —the offices of *The Miami News*—we were told the building was inspired by the Giralda in Seville. That's in Spain.

PEDRO: *(To* SOCORRO*)* I think he knows where Seville is!

SOCORRO: *(To* PEDRO*)* What if he didn't?

PEDRO *clears his throat to quiet his wife.*

LÍA: Anyway, from there we took the trolley and went shopping at Burdines—

PEDRO: —where they got that espresso machine.

SOCORRO: Don't interrupt her!

FIDEL *and* LÍA *laugh.*

FIDEL: So you're shopping ... and ...

LÍA: And we're just tourists, walking around, but completely oblivious to what was really going on. *(Pauses, looks directly at him)* Alejandro, we were blind to the reality of the United States!

FIDEL: What do you mean you were blind?

SOCORRO: Answer him truthfully!

FIDEL: Yes, Lía, I always want you to speak the truth to me, no matter what it is.

LÍA: We were in Miami, going shopping, and then we decided to go get some milkshakes. So we walked over to the Woolworth store. And we sat at the counter and ordered milkshakes—strawberry and vanilla.

She pauses. SOCORRO *looks at her;* PEDRO *clears his throat.*

SOCORRO: And then ...

LÍA: Then my sister pointed out a sign that said, "Whites Only." And then she looked around said, "Here we are, foreign tourists in the United States, and because we're white, we can sit here and be served. But an American citizen, born in this country, who happens to be a Negro, won't be served." I didn't know what to think. Then my sister went on, "What kind of country is this where visitors passing through have more rights than the people who were born here?"

SOCORRO: After that, we noticed all the signs posted everywhere: On the trolley, we could sit in the front, but not the back. When we walked down Biscayne Boulevard, the moment a Negro man or woman approached us, they had to stop, and step aside, letting us pass, even if they had to step onto the street. Water fountains, some for Whites, others for Negros. Same with the restroom facilities. Even at Burdines, when we went to store café for tea, all the servers were Negros dressed in uniforms who looked down and never, ever once looked us in the eyes.

LÍA: My sister wanted to go to the Key West, but we were—

FIDEL:—what? You were what?

PEDRO: They were scared, Alejandro. They were scared.

LÍA: That experience at Woolworth changed everything for us.

A silence hangs over the Cámara family. FIDEL *clears his throat softly. The awkward moment is broken.*

SOCORRO: Coffee? *(To* PEDRO, *nudging his elbow)* Ready to come help?

PEDRO: Yes! Yes! Of course I am!

PEDRO *and* SOCORRO *exit.*

FIDEL: Do you see now?

LÍA: See what?

FIDEL: How the world is full of injustice. And why that's why we have an obligation to right the wrongs we see.

LÍA; But what can one person do? *(*FIDEL'S *hand reaches for her shoulders)* I think I'm doing the best to make things better, as I teacher. But that's such a small contribution.

FIDEL: If in a country as large as the United States—

LÍA:—"El monstruo," as José Martí called it ...

They laugh.

FIDEL: The monster's entrails are entangled in racism and injustice, Lía. I have been to New York, Philadelphia, and even Miami—I have witnessed the oppression of the Negro race at the hands of Yankee Imperialist racists. I have seen the great injustices the American capitalist system imposes on its own people—and on the peoples of other nations. We must resist the empty promises of material comfort if those material comforts are secured through moral depravity and the oppression of others.

LÍA: *(Changing the subject)* Let's go see a movie, Mr. Philosopher.

FIDEL: A movie?

LÍA: Yes! I want to forget about this world of ours! Movies do that, take you away for a while.

FIDEL: A picnic and a movie on the same day?

LÍA: Does this mean we're getting serious?

FIDEL: I'm nothing but serious!

LÍA: About what?

FIDEL: *(Smiling, moving close to her)* About you.

LÍA: *(Flattered, embarrassed)* About me?

FIDEL: Of course about you, Lía. *(Pause)* I've fallen for you.

LÍA: *(Resisting as he tries to embrace her)* "Ensayo de un Crimen" is showing at the movie house downtown. Let's go see it.

Fidel: *(Holding her, and then closer)* Whatever you want.

LÍA: It's his latest film. *(She speaks slower as FIDEL tightens his hold around her waist)* Want to see it? It's supposed to be his best!

FIDEL: *(Indifferent)* Whose?

LÍA: Luis Buñuel.

FIDEL: *(Indifferent)* Oh?

LÍA: It's about a would-be serial killer.

FIDEL: *(Focusing on her)* Sounds lovely.

LÍA: But I don't think he carries out the murders he plans.

FIDEL: *(Oblivious to everything else but her)* Sounds lovely.

FIDEL *reaches and kisses her on the lips. She resists momentarily, then surrenders. After they kiss, she slowly moves back.*

LÍA: Yesterday, you kissed me at the restaurant. And now, in my home. *(Flirting)* Is this going to become a habit of yours?

FIDEL: Would that be such a bad thing?

We hear the commotion of LÍA'S *parents returning.* LÍA *is startled and moves away from* FIDEL. SOCORRO *enters carrying a tray with coffee cups, spoons, and a sugar bowl.* PEDRO *carries white cloth napkins.*

SOCORRO: Coffee?
FIDEL: That would be great.

SOCORRO *offers* FIDEL *and her daughter coffee. They take the small espresso cups.* LÍA *adds sugar;* FIDEL *does not.*

LÍA: Yes, Mother, thank you for making coffee.
PEDRO: I helped!
LÍA: Thank you as well, Father.
PEDRO: Thanks accepted.
FIDEL: Would it be alright with you, Don Pedro, if your daughter and I go to the movies this evening?
PEDRO: If she hasn't tired of your already, why not?
SOCORRO: Pedro!
LÍA: Father!
(The men laugh.)
SOCORRO: Honestly, Pedro. Have you manners? *(To* FIDEL*)* Not that you need our permission, Alejandro, but you two kids go and have fun.
LÍA: Thanks!

Suddenly, the music stops. PEDRO *raises his finger before speaking.*

PEDRO: Your sister's done with her practice. That means it's six o'clock.
FIDEL: What time is the movie?
LÍA: Eight.
FIDEL: That gives enough time to go back to my hotel, freshen up, and be back to pick you up. *(To* LÍA'S *parents)* If you'll excuse me.
FIDEL *places his espresso cup on the tray.*
PEDRO: Go on, be on your way, young man.
FIDEL *exits.*

LÍA: I need to get ready as well!
PEDRO: No surprise there!
LÍA *puts her espresso cup down and exits.*
PEDRO: Do you think they like each other?
SOCORRO: *(Giving him a look)* What do you think?
PEDRO: That maybe they do.
SOCORRO: *(Lightly hitting him atop his head)* No kidding!
PEDRO: What movie are they going to see?
SOCORRO: She's been talking about the new film by Luis Buñuel.
PEDRO: That surrealist?
SOCORRO: Yes, why?
PEDRO: Why can't they go see a comedy? These surrealist films, all that thinking about what—existentialism? Nihilism? I don't get it. *(Pause)* What's it called?
SOCORRO: I read about it in the paper. It's "The Criminal Life of Archibaldo de la Cruz."
PEDRO: The criminal life? *(Sarcastically)* Wonderful! What's that mess—I mean—movie about?
SOCORRO: It's something about this man who wants to be a serial killer and he practices over and over again about how he'd go about doing it.
PEDRO: Really?
SOCORRO: Really.
PEDRO: The movies, these days. Honestly.
SOCORRO: *(Shrugging her shoulders)* What can I say?
PEDRO: What you can say is that you agree with me and that they should go see a comedy! What's wrong with Cantinflas?
SOCORRO: They're too smart for slapstick comedy.
PEDRO: Luis Buñuel?
SOCORRO: *(Shrugging her shoulders)* Yes, Luis Buñuel. *(Pause)* Is there something wrong with that?
PEDRO: That man makes the kinds of films that only a person who lost his homeland to a dictator can make. Macabre and despondent! *(Pause)* And that's entertainment?

Scene 7

Mérida, Mexico. 1956

The Cámara family residence. PEDRO CÁMARA *is having coffee with* FIDEL CASTRO, *who is smoking a cigarette. There is a small suitcase by the door; it belongs to* FIDEL. *Offstage we hear "Wanderer" Fantasy in C major by Franz Schubert;* LÍA CÁMARA'S *sister is practicing her piano.*

PEDRO: I tell you, you're wrong, Alejandro.
FIDEL: I am not, Don Pedro. I am certain that I'm not.
PEDRO: The world—*as life*—is very complicated. Insisting on one single solution is—
FIDEL:—stubborn?
PEDRO: No, Alejandro. It's not being stubborn.
FIDEL: Then what?
PEDRO: It's being dogmatic.
FIDEL: Is that wrong?
PEDRO: It's not just wrong; it's deadly.
FIDEL: Deadly?
PEDRO: Oh, yes! It is deadly!
FIDEL: How?
PEDRO: *(Laughing)* How? How can you ask such a question? *(Pause)* Listen my son, dogmas do away with the possibility of ... *extenuating* circumstances, for one.
FIDEL: Extenuating circumstances?
PEDRO: Yes, you know. Exceptions. *(Pause, then in jest)* Didn't you tell me you have a law degree?
FIDEL: Yes.
PEDRO: It's what the law calls Force Majeure, no?
FIDEL: I see what you're saying.
PEDRO: But do you get it? *(Pause)* It's possible to be intelligent to the point of becoming unreasonable.
SOCORRO *enters carrying a tray with cold beverages.*
SOCORRO: Raised voices! In my house! *(Pause)* Any voice that drowns out the glorious music of Franz Schubert is

forbidden!

The men laugh.

PEDRO: Then tell Alejandro to come to his senses and agree with me!

SOCORRO: Agree with you? *(Laughing)* That requires a leap of faith!

SOCORRO *puts down the tray and hands the men glasses of the cold tea beverages.* PEDRO *hands* FIDEL *and his wife cloth napkins.*

PEDRO: A leap of faith! *(In an accusatory manner)* So you doubt my having any sense?

She gives him a look; FIDEL *laughs.*

FIDEL: Should I be prudent and doubt Don Pedro?

PEDRO: Only if you want to be as misguided in your reasoning as a woman, Alejandro!

SOCORRO: Pedro Cámara Lara! You take that back! I will not have you mock womanhood that way! Not under this roof! Not in this day and age!

PEDRO: Okay, okay! *(To* SOCORRO*)* You know you're my Angel of Reason! *(To* FIDEL, *rolling his eyes)* Don't ever make fun of a woman!

SOCORRO: Angel of Reason!

PEDRO: Which is why I'm glad you're here.

SOCORRO: You are?

PEDRO: Yes, because you can help me reason with this unreasonable young man—

SOCORRO:—about what?

PEDRO: About life.

SOCORRO: About life?

PEDRO: Yes, about life. *(Pointing to* FIDEL*)* Alejandro talks a big game about everything in the world being black or white—and he forgets the many shades of gray.

SOCORRO: Well, you do have a point about that, I have to admit.

PEDRO: *(To* FIDEL*)* See, Alejandro, even my wife agrees with me!

FIDEL: That might be true for some things—

PEDRO:—for almost *all* things! *(With impatience)* There are

always shades of gray in life, Alejandro!
FIDEL: Not so, Don Pedro. *(Lawyerly)* Two plus two is always four, and there's no room for debate about that! The sun rises in the east and sets in the west, and there's no room for debate about that either!
SOCORRO: He does have a point.
PEDRO: *(Annoyed)* Don't take his side! No one's disputing scientific and mathematic facts, but when it comes to society—political, cultural, and social things—there's room for opinions and choices and changes of ideas!
FIDEL: I'm not so sure about that. I believe that human progress is a didactic that leads us down a single path to social perfection.
PEDRO: *(Annoyed)* That's a very presumptuous claim to make.
FIDEL: Friedrich Engels made that claim.
PEDRO: I can make the claim the world is flat! But making a claim does not make it correct.
SOCORRO: *(With humor)* So glad I brought some cold drinks to cool things off!
PEDRO: *(Annoyed)* Are you saying I'm a hothead?
FIDEL: *(Chuckling)* No one is saying that, Don Pedro.
SOCORRO: *(To* FIDEL*)* God spare you a father-in-law like this man!
FIDEL: No, Doña Socorro. *(To* PEDRO*)* Any man would be happy to have Don Pedro as an in-law.
PEDRO: *(To* LÍA*)*There's no room for debate on that point!
The three laugh. The doorbell rings.
SOCORRO: Who can that be?
She exits.
PEDRO: *(In an avuncular fashion)* You need to understand two things, Alejandro.
FIDEL: About?
PEDRO: About life! *(Pause)* The first is that it's possible to be too intelligent. And the other is that one can never forget compassion.
FIDEL: Compassion is relative; a strict father is more compassionate than one who indulges his child's every

whim.

PEDRO: True, compassion can take many forms.

FIDEL: And intelligence?

PEDRO: Yes, there are many ways of being smart—and even more ways of going nuts. *(Pause)* In fact, remember, a curse accompanies intelligence.

FIDEL: *(Laughing)* A curse? Now you're sounding like an old, black Cuban lady who believes in the foolishness of Santería!

PEDRO: *(Shaking his head)* You can doubt all you want, Alejandro, but there is a curse that comes with being very intelligent.

FIDEL: And that would be—

PEDRO:—the specter of insanity!

FIDEL *laughs.* SOCORRO *returns. She is holding an armful of marigold flowers.*

SOCORRO: What's so funny?

PEDRO: What's with those flowers?

FIDEL: Don Pedro made a joke—that intelligent people run the risk of going crazy.

PEDRO: It's not a joke.

SOCORRO: A flower lady.

PEDRO: What?

SOCORRO: The flowers. *(As she walks to a vase on a table with the flowers)* A Maya lady was selling flowers for the dead.

PEDRO: It's coming up already!

SOCORRO: All Souls' Day, All Saints' Day, Day of the Dead. All Hallows' Eve. *(To* FIDEL*)* Fall does that to you, a time to reflect.

PEDRO: *(To* FIDEL*)* And if you reflect thoughtfully, you come to the realization that intelligence, in excess, leads to insanity.

SOCORRO: *(To* FIDEL*)* He's right, Alejandro.

FIDEL: Don't tell me you believe such nonsense, Doña Socorro!

SOCORRO: Well, he does have a point!

PEDRO: Thank you for being reasonable, my dear. *(To*

FIDEL) In fact, there's a perfect case in point not far from here. That boy, *(pausing)* ...
SOCORRO: Who?
PEDRO: The brilliant one, the prodigy.
SOCORRO: Chess?
PEDRO: Yes, him. What's his name?
SOCORRO: Carlos Torre.
PEDRO: That's right! *(To* FIDEL*)* Carlos Torre, as a boy, was a chess prodigy—chess is very big around here—and he's on his way to becoming a grandmaster!
FIDEL: That means he's intelligent—
SOCORRO: —but he's also losing his mind, Alejandro.
LÍA *enters the room. She walks over to* FIDEL *and kisses him on his cheek. He puts his arm around her waist.*
LÍA: *(Smiling)* Who are you talking about?
PEDRO: That crazy Carlos Torre—
SOCORRO: —he's not crazy.
PEDRO: Not yet, but he will be.
FIDEL *and* LÍA *laugh.*
LÍA: *(To* FIDEL, *playfully)* Please take me to Mexico City with you so I can get away from these two!
PEDRO: *(To* LÍA*)* Don't mock your old man! *(To* FIDEL*)* It's like that woman we read about who married the crazy American.
SOCORRO: Aren't they all crazy in the U.S.?
PEDRO: Let me correct myself: the super-intelligent and crazy American.
SOCORRO: Who?
LÍA: *(Smiling)* I think he means Alicia. Alicia Lardé.
PEDRO: Yes! That one! *(To* FIDEL*)* Another case in point, Alejandro. Alicia Lardé makes the mistake of falling in love with a brilliant American—so it's no surprise that the brilliant American, that Professor Nash, is crazy!
SOCORRO: Isn't he a mathematician? John Nash? *(Pause)* Poor Alicia, stuck with an insane American for a husband!
PEDRO: And mathematics is just like chess!
LÍA: And music! *(Pointing her finger)* If my sister keeps

playing like that, according to Father, she'll go crazy.
PEDRO: Mozart was crazy! *(Pause)* Good thing we no longer have brilliant composers.
SOCORRO: The ones today aren't intelligent enough?
PEDRO: As a matter of fact they've been so medicated with tranquilizers that they stay sane—and as such their work is hardly brilliant. No one alive today compares with Mozart, Beethoven, Chopin! I could go on!
SOCORRO: And go on you do!
PEDRO: *(To* FIDEL*)* Now, getting back to Carlos Torre. Back in 1925 at the Moscow Chess Tournament, he defeated world chess champion Emanuel Lasker!
FIDEL: Really?
PEDRO: Oh, yes, it was a brilliant queen sacrifice. *(Pausing)* The combination is known as "The Windmill." In fact, I have it written down.

PEDRO *walks to* FIDEL *who lets go of* LÍA'S *waist.* PEDRO *takes* FIDEL *by the elbow and the men being to exit.* LÍA *walks to her mother.*

PEDRO: "The Windmill" is the product of exceptional intelligence—which is why I say that Carlos is going crazy. Only a madman would think of ever sacrificing his queen. *(Pause)* Now that I think about it, there was a Cuban at the tournament in Moscow: José Raúl Capablanca. Have you ever heard of him?
FIDEL: *(Quietly to* PEDRO*, as the men walk to the door)* I don't know who he is.

The men exit.

LÍA: Isn't he dreamy?
SOCORRO: He's a wonderful young man.
LÍA: How can anyone not fall for him?
SOCORRO: He's quite something. *(Lighthearted)* And to think you met him on a public bus! Maybe your sister should start riding buses across the peninsula back and forth!
LÍA: Stop being ridiculous! *(Pause)* Next year, when I turn twenty-one, I might be ready—
SOCORRO: *(Turning to* LÍA*, sternly)*—ready for what?

LÍA: Mother! It's time I thought about marriage and starting a family. Alejandro is—
SOCORRO:—A DIVORCED MAN WITH A SON!
LÍA: *(Defiantly)* Well, I don't care!
SOCORRO: *(Sternly)* But we do! Your father has been very understanding—
LÍA:—considering he was born in 1899!
SOCORRO: Nevertheless, he's very modern, Lía. It did surprise him when you told him Alejandro is divorced, but your Father has not stood in your way!
LÍA: I know. *(Humbled)* And I am grateful to both of you for falling for him as well.
SOCORRO: Yes, but he is *still* a divorced man with a son—and that concerns me—
LÍA: Then don't *you* marry him! But *I* will!
SOCORRO: You're getting ahead of yourself, Lía. *(Pause)* He's leaving for Mexico City again, and you haven't even met his family.
LÍA: I met his brother, Raúl. He was here last time. They went driving all over the place. He's a short little guy with a funny moustache, baby brother Raúl.
SOCORRO: Well, meeting his baby brother, as you say, is not the same thing as meeting his parents—or his son. Have you considered the responsibility of being a stepmother? *(Pause)* How long have you known him? Just over a year—in his comings and goings to Mexico City. *(Pause)* My darling, we want you to be happy, Lía. But we want you to be smart.
LÍA: Careful, Mother! If I'm too smart, according to Father, I'll end up crazy!
The women laugh. We hear the men as they enter.
PEDRO: Did I miss a joke?
SOCORRO: No, no joke. *(Looking at* FIDEL, *then* LÍA. *To* PEDRO*)* Please be a dear and come help me in the kitchen.
PEDRO: *(Looking at* LÍA *and* FIDEL, *and getting it)* Of course! Aren't you making a sandwich for Alejandro to take on the plane?

SOCORRO: As a matter of fact, nothing they serve on any airplane can compete with my cooking!

They chuckle as they exit.

FIDEL: *(Smiling)* Your parents are wonderful.

LÍA: They're fond of you, Alejandro.

FIDEL *turns serious; his demeanor becomes somber.*

FIDEL: I have something to tell you—or rather, explain to you.

LÍA: *(Apprehensive)* What? What is it? Is something wrong?

FIDEL: *(He puts his finger to her lips, in a calming voice)* Nothing is wrong, Lía. But this trip I'm taking is not like the others.

LÍA: *(Stepping back)* What do you mean?

FIDEL: LET ME explain.

LÍA: Go on.

FIDEL: You, more than any history book, have taught me that patriots are men of action who must be prepared to do what must be done for the greater good.

LÍA: Yes, but what does that have to do with you—with us?

FIDEL: That I love you—but I also love Cuba. And as a man—a man of action—I want you to know that I do love you. But as a patriot, I have to go back to Cuba and be the patriot my country needs.

LÍA: Be a patriot?

FIDEL: I have to do *one* thing for my country—and then I will send for you.

LÍA: Send for me?

FIDEL: I may not be able to come back here myself, and if that's the case, I will send for you.

LÍA: I don't understand.

Suddenly, the music stops, indicating it is six o'clock and LÍA'S *sister has stopped her music practice for the day.*

FIDEL: *(Taking her hand)* I am in love with you, Lía.

LÍA: *(Doubting)* Are you?

FIDEL: Yes.

LÍA: Send for me? I still don't understand.

FIDEL *reaches over and kisses* LÍA. *The lovers embrace. Then* FIDEL *steps back, and holds her hand.*

FIDEL: I am leaving only because I have to leave. Not because I want to leave. Remember what José Martí once said.
LÍA: He said many things, Alejandro. Many beautiful things.
FIDEL: Well, one of his beautiful sayings was, "We light the oven so that everyone may bake bread in it."
LÍA *looks away.* SOCORRO *enters. She is carrying a paper bag with food for* FIDEL.
SOCORRO: It's already six! *(To* FIDEL*)* We have to leave for the airport, Alejandro. *(To* LÍA*)* Your father went to get the car. Are you going to the airport with us?
FIDEL: No, no she's not.
SOCORRO: *(To* LÍA*)* You're not?
LÍA: No, Mother. Alejandro's right. If I went, I think I would cry.
SOCORRO: *(To* LÍA*)* Cry? But why?
FIDEL: I'm leaving for Mexico City, Doña Socorro, but then I'm going to Cuba for a while.
SOCORRO: Oh, that's wonderful! I'm sure your son misses you! *(To* LÍA*)* Wouldn't it be great to visit Havana, Lía. Especially after the frightful experience in Miami!
LÍA: Yes, Mother! *(To* FIDEL*)* We can visit Cuba at any time!
FIDEL: Of course you can—and you will!
We hear a car honking.
SOCORRO: That's Pedro! I'll go and tell him to stop honking. *(Holding the paper bag up)* I've made something for your flight!
She rushes out, carrying the paper bag.
LÍA: You're not just saying you'll be back. You *will* be back, right?
FIDEL: *(Holding her hand)* If I cannot come back for you myself, then I will send for you.
He kisses her hand, then her cheek; she smiles.
LÍA: I'll be counting the days.
FIDEL: So will I.
We hear a car honking. FIDEL *walks over, picks up his suitcase, turns around, and blows her a kiss. He exits.*
LÍA: Adios, Alejandro.

Scene 8

Mexico City. 1956

A small apartment in Mexico City. FIDEL CASTRO *is smoking a cigarette, seated at a writing desk.* CHE GUEVARA *is pacing the room. It is sparsely furnished. There are two large maps on the wall, one of Cuba and one of Mexico. There are beer bottles, bottles of rum, stacks of paper, and books about. Clothes are strewn all over the place.* FIDEL *is reading.* RAÚL CASTRO *walks in.*

RAÚL: It's all set.
FIDEL: *(Moving to the window, moving the curtain with discretion)* The show we've been putting on for our friends across the street is about to end.
RAÚL: And our show in Cuba is about to begin.
CHE: *(Bouncing around the apartment with exuberance and energy)* Yes! Revolución! It's time for men of action to act! It's time for the capitalist filth suffocating the Cuban nation to be exterminated like an infestation! Next stop, Yucatán!
RAÚL: Not quite.
CHE: What do you mean?
RAÚL *reaches for his inside pocket and takes out three envelopes.*
RAÚL: Remember? Misdirection. Misinformation. Deception. *(Pause)* For months we have been watched, followed. The spies across the street know how many times we have been to the Yucatán. Now that they believe our propaganda, it is time to deceive them.
CHE: Deceive them?
FIDEL: *(Standing up)* The Yucatán is filled with Batista's spies—
RAÚL: —and the CIA.
FIDEL: *(Walking to* CHE*)* He's right. The CIA.
RAÚL: *(Handing an envelope to* CHE*)* Veracruz.

CHE: Veracruz?

FIDEL: What do you always say about passion?

CHE: *(Reciting from memory)* Passion is needed for any great work, and for the revolution, passion and audacity are required in big doses.

RAÚL: This is your bus ticket to Veracruz. We are assembling tonight, tomorrow, and the day after. Then we will set off for Cuba.

CHE: *(Looking at his bus ticket)* How many men? The final count?

FIDEL: The three of us here, plus seventy-nine more.

RAÚL: Cortés defeated the Aztec empire with a few hundred Spaniards. We will defeat Batista with a few dozen—

CHE: *(Bouncing about the room)*—men of action!

RAÚL: I'm flying to Tampico and then taking the bus down to Veracruz. *(Handing an envelope to FIDEL)* You will take the bus to Minatitlán, and then take a bus to Veracruz. Then we will all meet up in Tuxpan, and from there, we set sail for Cuba.

CHE: *(Moving to the window, moving the curtain with discretion)* They'll never know.

FIDEL: Che, you leave now.

CHE *picks up his coat, a small bag, placing books and papers inside.*

RAÚL: We cannot take anything from here. We each have to leave separately—and as if we were going to a café around the corner.

CHE: *(With tremendous enthusiasm)* The adventure begins!

CHE *bounces over and hugs* RAÚL, *who kisses him atop the head, and then he hugs* FIDEL.

RAÚL: *Patria o Muerte.* Country or death.

FIDEL: Next year, Havana!

CHE: *(With tremendous enthusiasm) Hasta la Victoria, siempre!* Until victory, always!

He grabs his coat and exits.

RAÚL: I have one errand to run, to say good-bye to a friend, and then I'll go straight to the airport, Fidel.

FIDEL: Go.

RAÚL: I'll see you in Veracruz.
FIDEL: Yes, you will. *(The brothers embrace. RAÚL picks up a small bag, his coat, and walks to the door.)*
RAÚL: We will be triumphant.

RAÚL *exits.* FIDEL *slowly walks around the room, turning off the lights. He reaches into his pocket and takes out his identification papers. He stares at them, then tears them to pieces. He tosses the them on the floor. He walks over to his desk and picks up a black-and-white photograph of* LÍA *and stares at it for a moment. He puts the photograph in his inside breast pocket as he puts on his coat and hat. He slowly and silently walks to the door, turns off the last light, and opens the door, taking one last look around.*

FIDEL: *(As he closes the door behind him)* Adios, Alejandro.

Scene 9

Mérida, Mexico. 1959

The Cámara family residence. There are New Year decorations throughout: party hats, confetti on the floor, balloons. A banner reads "Happy New Year 1959!" LÍA CÁMARA *holds a tray and is collecting champagne flutes. Her mother is sweeping confetti.*

PEDRO: *(Rushing into the room, holding newspapers)* Socorro! Lía!
SOCORRO: What's the matter?
PEDRO: *(Holding up the newspapers, frantic)* It's in the newspapers! Turn on the television! Turn it on!
LÍA: What's going on, Father?
PEDRO: *(Stopping to catch his breath, holding the newspapers so the front page is visible)* Revolution in Cuba! *(Turning to his daughter)* I want Lía to see this! *(To* SOCORRO*)* Turn on the television.
LÍA *puts down the tray and rushes over to see the newspaper.* SOCORRO *turns on the television.*
LÍA: I don't believe it!
PEDRO: It's him!
SOCORRO: Him who?
PEDRO: Look at the television!
The three stop, mesmerized by the television. We see a newsreel announcing that Cuban dictator Fulgencio Batista has fled Havana and FIDEL *declares victory. The vintage black-and-white news footage is a throwback to the early news broadcasts familiar in the late 1950s and early 1960s.*
SOCORRO: Revolution in Cuba? *(She makes the sign of the cross)* Batista has fled!
PEDRO: And look! Look who it is! *(Grabbing the newspaper from Lía's hands, and opening to a page inside, holding it up)* Look! Look who it is!

LÍA: Alejandro!
SOCORRO: Alejandro? What are you saying?
PEDRO: *(Visibly furious)* Not Alejandro González!
SOCORRO: What?
PEDRO: *(Enraged)* That man, we welcomed in our home, is Fidel Castro!
LÍA: No, it can't be! It can't be, Father!
SOCORRO: Oh, my heavens!
PEDRO: *(Enraged)* And you held out the hope that he'd come back for you, Lía? That man was a liar! He used you! He deceived us! He's *never* coming back for you!
LÍA: No, Father, Alejandro is a good man! I know it!
PEDRO: *(Yelling)* There's no such man as Alejandro González! Don't you understand?
LÍA: No, Father! You're wrong!
SOCORRO: Pedro!
PEDRO: What?
SOCORRO *points to her daughter.*
PEDRO: *(Quietly)* Alejandro González doesn't exist, my sweet daughter.
LÍA: *(In tears)* I don't believe it!
She rushes out of the room; SOCORRO *rushes over to her husband.*
SOCORRO: A revolution? Alejandro González is Fidel Castro? How? How? How is this possible?
PEDRO: *(Quietly)* Our poor daughter has been deceived.
SOCORRO: Worse.
PEDRO: Oh?
SOCORRO: Our little girl's heart has just been broken.

END OF ACT I

Act II

Scene 1

Mérida, Mexico 1959

Several months later. The Cámara family residence. We hear Piano Sonata No. 32 in C minor by Ludwig Van Beethoven in the background, offstage. LÍA CÁMARA *is sitting at a desk, preparing lesson plans. Her father,* PEDRO CÁMARA, *is reading the newspaper. The photograph taken at the beach is framed, resting on the table.* LÍA *is dusting the frame as* PEDRO *walks in.*

PEDRO: Again? How many times a day do you dust that photo?
LÍA: As many as I want to!
PEDRO: That must be the cleanest picture frame in the world!
LÍA: It's all I have of him. *(Picking up the frame)* I love that he's wearing mother's scarf.
PEDRO: Oh, that's right. That Grace Kelly scarf. *(Laughing)* Maybe he can wear it when he's giving his revolutionary speeches in Havana.
LÍA: *(She kisses the frame and puts it back down, then sternly)* Being cynical doesn't help.

We hear the doorbell ring.

SOCORRO: *(Offstage)* I'll get it.
PEDRO: Who could that be?
LÍA: I'm not expecting anyone.
SOCORRO: *(Walking in, holding a letter)* It's a special delivery for you, Lía.
LÍA: For me?
SOCORRO: It's by courier.
PEDRO: *(Putting down his newspaper, standing up)* By courier?
SOCORRO: *(Looking at* PEDRO *as she walks to her daughter, who looks up)* That's what I said, Pedro.

LÍA: *(Reaching for the letter)* Thank you, Mother. *(Looking at the envelope)* It's from the Cuban Consulate.

She stands up and opens the envelope. PEDRO *walks to his daughter and wife.*

PEDRO: What do the Cubans want with you?

SOCORRO: If you let her read the letter, we'll find out, won't we?

PEDRO: I hope it's not from that man!

LÍA: I'm not angry at Alejandro any more—

PEDRO: *(Adamant)*—it's Fidel! Fidel Castro, the man who lied to you, to your Mother, and to me!

SOCORRO: Leave the matter alone, Pedro.

LÍA *opens the letter and reads it in silence.*

PEDRO: What does it say?

LÍA: *(Reading the letter)* My dearest Lía, it is my hope that this letter finds you, your parents, and your sister well. When we last spoke I told you I had to do something for my country, Cuba. And I have. But I also made a promise to you: that if I could not return for you myself, I would send for you. And I am a man of my word. I have kept my word to Cuba and I am now keeping my word to you. It has taken some months to settle things, but my position is now secure and I have the mass support of the Cuban people. It is my hope that you understand that I did what I had to do to succeed in my duty as a patriot, a man of action, and a leader. I have freed Cuba from the bondage of tyranny. I ask you now to come to Havana. I have ordered the Cuban Consulate in Mérida to make all the necessary arrangements for you to come and be here with me. My love, please come back to me. Your Alejandro.

PEDRO: *(Adamant)* Fidel!

SOCORRO: *(Looking at* PEDRO*)* Pedro! *(To* LÍA*)* You are crazy if you accept that man's invitation, Lía.

Looking at the letter intensely.

PEDRO: Listen to your Mother, Lía. *(Pause)* That man lied to all of us!

LÍA: He had to do what he had to do.

PEDRO: *(Adamant)* Deceive us? Lie to us? Betray your affection for him? He had to do that?
SOCORRO: Your Father is right, Lía. You cannot go to Cuba.
LÍA: *(Looking up)* Cannot go to Cuba? *(Pause)* But I must go to Cuba!
PEDRO: *(Enraged)* What?
SOCORRO: *(Making a sign of the cross, shaking her head)* Oh, my dear, you cannot be serious!
PEDRO: But why? Why would you want to go?
LÍA: (Looking first at her Father then at her Mother. She picks up the framed photograph, the memento of their trip to the beach, and looks at it) Because I love him.

Scene 2

Santa Isabel de las Lajas, Cienfuegos Province, Cuba.
1961

A balcony overlooking a central plaza in a small town in rural Cuba—Revolutionary Cuba. French doors open onto the balcony. Cuban flags are draped on the doors and over the balcony. CHE GUEVARA *addresses a multitude. We hear chants of "Che!" He basks in the adulation of the crowd.*

CHE: Viva Cuba! Viva La Revolución!
We hear the crowd repeating the chants: "Viva Cuba!" and "Viva Fidel!" Then we hear a thunderous chorus of chants: "Che!" "Che!" "Che!"
CHE: We have delivered you from tyranny! We have delivered you from the Imperialism's bondage to a Yankee master! We have delivered to you a free and sovereign Cuba!
We hear the crowd repeating the chants: "Cuba!" and "Fidel!" interspersed with a chorus of chants: "Che!" "Che!" "Che!" Che Guevara basks in the adulation.
CHE: The Revolutionary Government is committed to the workers of Cuba! We stand united with the people against common enemies, common enemies that have strangled Cuba for decades for the economic benefit of Yankee Imperialists and the international Jewish bankers' conspiracy that is behind all oppression in the world today! We are in the processing of cleansing Cuba of Jewish swine and capitalist pigs, sending them all into exile, ending their oppression of the common man!
A chorus of "Che!" "Che!" "Che!" rises.
CHE: If you tremble with indignation at every injustice, then you are a comrade of mine! If you want Cuba free of American Imperialism, then you are a comrade of mine!
A chorus of "Che!" "Che!" "Che!" rises.

Scene 3

Havana, Cuba. 1959

An office in the Vedado district of Havana. It is an ample room with two desks, several cabinets, and chairs. There are documents stacked all over. There is a photograph of nineteenth century Cuban liberator and poet José Martí. There are photographs of Vladimir Lenin and Mao Zedong. A Cuban flag is prominently displayed. FIDEL CASTRO *stands by doors that open onto a balcony. He is slowly waving, basking in the adulation of the public. We hear shouts of "Fidel! Fidel! Fidel!"* LÍA CÁMARA, *welcomed to Havana as a Revolutionary Hero, is in* FIDEL'S *inner circle. She opens the door from where* FIDEL'S *aides and staff are working, and quietly walks into the office. She stares at him, with admiration. Then she speaks.*

LÍA: Alejandro.
FIDEL *slowly turns around and sees* LÍA. *He smiles as he admires her, then turns away from the open doors looking onto the balcony. The Cuban public's adulation fades; she is all he sees.*
FIDEL: Lía! You're here!
They walk to each other.
LÍA: Of course I'm here! Didn't you send for me?
FIDEL: Yes, but I wasn't sure if—
LÍA:—if I'd come.
FIDEL: If you would forgive me.
LÍA: Yes. *(Pause, extending her hand, which he takes and clasps)* We can talk about that later, Mr. González.
FIDEL: Then you still love me, despite . . .
LÍA: Yes, I love you more than I'm angry with you.
He reaches over and kisses her; they embrace. After a moment, they step back to take it all in again, making sure it is real. Then, there is a second hug, this one stronger and much longer, when all the weight and

memory of separation vanish.
FIDEL: It's so wonderful to hold you again.
LÍA: It's just as wonderful to be held!
FIDEL: Thank you for the chocolates.
LÍA: You got them? I wasn't sure if you'd get them. I just dropped them off at the Consulate.
FIDEL: They know that anything from you comes to me without delay. *(Pause)* Chocolates. You remembered.
They move comfortably as lovers do when delighted to be back together.
LÍA: How could I forget? It was part of my "Miami misadventure."
FIDEL: That's right, that's right. *(Pause)* When you, your Mother, and sister went for milkshakes at Woolworth—
LÍA: —we ordered vanilla and strawberry, but not chocolate.
FIDEL: Yes, not chocolate! As Don Pedro said *(imitating* PEDRO*)*, "Americans don't understand chocolate the same way they don't understand coffee! They make terrible chocolate! If you want good chocolate, you get Mexican chocolate—where chocolate originates."
LÍA: He trusts Americans with strawberries and vanilla—
FIDEL: —even if vanilla also comes from Mexico!
They laugh—and look at each other.
LÍA: Chocolate, vanilla, tomatoes, and avocados, Mexico's gifts to the world—
FIDEL: —and you.
LÍA: Me?
FIDEL: You, Lía, are Mexico's gift to the world. Or at least Mexico's gift to me.
He reaches over and kisses her on the cheek.
LÍA: *(Embarrassed)* Stop it, Alejandro.
FIDEL: It's Fidel. You know that.
LÍA: Well, to me, you'll always be Alejandro. That's the name I knew you by when I fell in love with you.
FIDEL: *(Whispering)* Then you can call me "Alejandro."
LÍA: *(Moving about, checking out the office)* If someone had told me that Alejandro González was a secret revolutionary—

FIDEL: —you would have what?

LÍA: *(Flirting)* I would have laughed. *(Moving her hands in a broad gesture)* But look at this! Look at where I am! It's real, isn't it?

FIDEL: Yes, it's real.

LÍA: But how?

FIDEL: *(Caressing her shoulder)* There will be time for that!

LÍA: All I know is what they've reporting in the news these past months—

FIDEL: —how we left Mexico an army of 82 men and how, a month later, we had been reduced to only fifteen fugitive rebels.

LÍA: *(Nodding, as he guides her around the office)* Yes! And how you were hunted by Batista's troops—

FIDEL: —hiding in the Sierra Maestra for months.

LÍA: Until—

FIDEL: *(Looking at her with affection)*— triumph was ours.

LÍA: And look at what you've done! You've liberated Cuba!

FIDEL: *(Moving his arm in a sweeping motion, gesturing at the room)* And now the work begins! *(Pause)* Over dinner, I'll tell you everything about how we carried out this triumph over tyranny!

LÍA: *(Looking around the office, with humility)* When Che and his men met me at the airport, it was as if a celebrity had arrived—Elizabeth Taylor, or Natalie Wood, or Princess Grace of Monaco—

FIDEL: —or you.

LÍA: Be serious, Alejandro.

FIDEL: *(Whispering)* I am serious, Lía.

LÍA: Well, I was embarrassed, the way people were staring at me. When Camilo Cienfuegos asked who I was, he said, "That's Lía Cámara, the future First Lady of Cuba."

FIDEL: Would that be such a bad thing?

LÍA: *(Blushing)* No—

FIDEL: *(Whispering)* Not really?

LÍA: Not really.

FIDEL: *(In a lighthearted manner)* Well, that's reassuring!

They laugh. The door opens and RAÚL *walks in.*

RAÚL: *(To* LÍA*)* I thought I heard your lovely voice, Lía. Welcome to a liberated Cuba!

He walks over to her, takes her hands, and kisses her hands.

LÍA: It's good to see you, Raúl.

RAÚL: First in Mérida, and now in Havana!

LÍA: *(With delight)* I'm thrilled to be in Cuba, a liberated Cuba! *(Pause, as she smiles at the* CASTRO *brothers)* Oh, Raúl, my sister sends you her regards.

RAÚL: Your beautiful sister! Who plays the piano with such flair and style!

FIDEL: *(To* RAÚL*)* Like the concert pianist that she is.

RAÚL: *(To* LÍA*)* Did Fidel thank you for the chocolates? *(To* FIDEL*)* They were for him, but I ate most of them!

The brothers laugh.

LÍA: I'm so happy to be with the two of you.

FIDEL: And I can't tell you how happy I am to have this teacher—*this great student of history*—here by my side once again. When I think of long evenings we spent talking about history, the world, its problems, and what needed to be done—

LÍA: —you think of the possibility of hope!

FIDEL: Yes, Lía. I think of the promise of this new day.

RAÚL: And I think of the important tasks that are before us.

FIDEL: Do you want to be a part of it?

LÍA: A part of what?

RAÚL: A part of Cuba's future.

LÍA: *(Surprised)* What?

FIDEL: You are a wonderful teacher, and Cuba needs teachers.

RAÚL: Let me ask you this, Lía. Under Batista, not much was done to educate people in rural communities.

FIDEL: Most Cuban peasants are illiterate.

RAÚL: And your experience with teaching Indians—

LÍA: —the Maya, Raúl, not "Indian."

RAÚL: Very well, the Maya—

FIDEL: —the point being, can you—

LÍA: —can I what?

FIDEL: Ask her, Raúl.
RAÚL: Can you help us set up a literacy program for rural communities?
LÍA: *(Astounded)* Do you think I can do that?
RAÚL: Why not?
LÍA: *(Surprised)* I mean, it's one thing to be a simple teacher—
FIDEL: *(Laughing)*—there's nothing simple about you, Lía!
RAÚL: Are you willing? Because if you are, I'll contact Celia Sánchez, and she can assist you.
FIDEL: Are you in?
LÍA: *(Smiling, glowing, and with confidence)* If you want me to, Alejandro, then I am in!
FIDEL: *(Reaching over and kissing her on the cheek)* Yes! A million times yes!
RAÚL: And the Cuban people will be forever grateful. *(Pause, looking at* FIDEL *first, then* LÍA*)* Then it's settled!
FIDEL: We will proclaim 1961 to be the Year of Education.
RAÚL: *La Campaña Nacional de Alfabetización en Cuba!*
FIDEL: From January 1, 1961 through the end of December, we will organize the most ambitious literacy campaign the world has ever known! 1961 will be the Year of Education—
RAÚL:—and that means we will need Literacy Brigades!
LÍA: Literacy Brigades?
RAÚL: Those in the cities who believe in justice are prepared to dedicate themselves to the Revolution—and Cuba. They will fan out throughout the countryside to teach peasants.
LÍA: Oh, my goodness! *(Raising her hand to her face)* That's a tall order!
FIDEL: Why?
LÍA: In Mexico, it took us in Mexico *decades* to get the education system going …
RAÚL: But we have two advantages in Cuba.
LÍA: We do?
FIDEL: Of course, Lía!

LÍA: And they are?

RAÚL: The first is that Cuban peasants speak only Spanish—so there's not obstacle posed by teaching them Spanish first.

LÍA: That's true.

RAÚL: And the second advantage is that we can build on Mexico's experience—

FIDEL:—reducing the Revolution's mistakes.

RAÚL: Can we do that?

LÍA: *(With growing confidence)* I believe we can do that!

FIDEL: Of course we can!

RAÚL: With your help!

LÍA: Yes, we can do it! *(Pause, then with confidence)* We will do it!

RAÚL: Educating the masses is crucial to the Revolution's success.

LÍA: Education is—

RAÚL:—political power!

FIDEL: Isn't she wonderful, Raúl?

RAÚL: You're a lucky man, Fidel. *(Slowly and sincerely)* One very lucky man.

LÍA: The Literacy Campaign will be a tremendous success, I promise you that, Alejandro.

RAÚL: Alejandro? *(Laughing)* She still calls you that, Fidel?

FIDEL: She can call me anything she wants.

Scene 4

Santa Isabel de las Lajas, Cienfuegos Province, Cuba. 1961

A balcony overlooking a central plaza in a small town in rural Havana. French doors open onto the balcony. Cuban flags are draped on the doors and over the balcony. CHE GUEVARA *addresses a multitude as* LÍA CÁMARA *watches. We hear chants of "Che!" He speaks to the public, basking in their adulation.*

CHE: Our every action is a battle cry against Imperialism, and a battle hymn for the people's unity against the great enemy of mankind: the United States of America. Wherever death may surprise us, let it be welcome, provided that this, our battle cry, may have reached some receptive ear, that another hand may be extended to wield our weapons, and that other men be ready to intone our funeral dirge with the staccato singing of the machine guns and new battle cries of war and victory.

A chorus of "Che!" "Che!" "Che!"rises.

CHE: I am not a liberator. Liberators do not exist. The people liberate themselves.

A chorus of "Che!" "Che!" "Che!"rises.

CHE: But now, with Fidel, we are reaching for common goals: social justice, independence, dignity!

A chorus of "Che!" "Che!" "Che!"rises.

CHE: To solidify Cuba's sovereignty, we need education! To read! To write! Education is power that will protect our Revolution from the bourgeois pawns of the Imperialists!

A chorus of "Che!" "Che!" "Che!"rises.

CHE: We have ended foreign domination of Cuba! We have ended the American Mafia's grip on our tourism industry, of our hotels, in our sugar industry, and throughout the tobacco fields! We *close* the casinos so

we can *open* schools!
A chorus of "Che!" "Che!" "Che!"rises.

CHE: The Revolutionary Government has declared 1961 to be the Year of Education! The Revolutionary Government has decreed the establishment of Literacy Brigades! The Revolutionary Government challenges the whole of Latin America to look to Cuba as a shining example! Let the whole of Latin America know that the great Cuban nation is standing firmly and proudly, as a great nation must!

A chorus of "Che!" "Che!" "Che!"rises.

CHE: Cuba today, Latin America tomorrow!

A chorus of "Che!" "Che!" "Che!"rises.

CHE: There are no boundaries in this struggle to the death. We cannot be indifferent to what happens anywhere in the world, for a victory by any country over Imperialism is our victory; just as any country's defeat is a defeat for all of us. And what better proof than the fact that I, an Argentine, stand here before you and with you!

A chorus of "Che!" "Che!" "Che!"rises.

CHE: And the Year of Education—its Literacy Brigades—a program to teach every Cuban to read and write is spearheaded by a Mexican teacher! That is proof of the love from all corners of the world for Cuba, for Fidel, for you!

A chorus of "Che!" "Che!" "Che!"rises.

CHE: From Mexico to Argentina, the whole of Latin America stands with Cuba!

A chorus of "Che!" "Che!" "Che!"rises.

CHE: The heart of the Cuban Revolution is alive in the bodies of men and women of goodwill from the world over! The heart of the Cuban Revolution beats in my chest and in the chest of this great Mexican teacher! Let me present to you the future First Lady of Cuba! It is my honor to present our comrade, Maestra Lía Cámara!

LÍA, *with confidence, steps up to the microphone as* CHE *steps aside. She looks at the multitudes, grips the railing, and addresses the Cuban people for the first time. A chorus of "Lía!" "Lía!" "Lía!" rises.*

LÍA: I am a humble Mexican citizen. But I am a friend of Cuba. And because I am a friend of Cuba and I have love for her people, I stand before you to make you one promise. *(Pause)* I promise to be here for you! I am a teacher! I will teach you to read! To write! I will teach you how to master the skills necessary to pursue your education!

A chorus of "Lía!" "Lia!" "Lía!" begins to rise.

LÍA: The Revolution bestows upon you the gift that is your birthright and which Batista denied you! *(Pause)* The Revolution bestows you the gift of the alphabet! The gift of reading! The gift of writing! The gift of knowledge!

A chorus of "Lía!" "Lía!" "Lía!" rises. CHE *smiles, encourages the crowd, and looks on approvingly.*

LÍA: Fidel has proclaimed 1961 as the Year of Education! And I, Lía Cámara, promise you here and now that the Literacy Brigades will not stop until every Cuban—no matter how humble or how far from Havana—is taught to read, to write, to think! Education is the Revolution's promise to you! It is Fidel's promise to you! And it is my promise to you! I will not stop until this promise is fulfilled!

A thunderous chorus of "Lía!" "Lia!" "Lía!" rises. CHE *returns to her side, raising her arm for all to see.*

CHE: The future First Lady of Cuba! The future of Cuba!

A thunderous chorus of "Lía!" "Lia!" "Lía!" rises.

Scene 5

Mérida, Mexico. 1961

The Cámara family residence. Offstage we hear Piano Sonato No. 15 "Pastoral" in D major by Ludwig Van Beethoven. PEDRO CÁMARA *is reading the newspaper as the music sounds throughout their living room. A doorbell rings.*

SOCORRO: *(Offstage)* I'll get it.
PEDRO: *(Not looking up)* Thanks, honey.
SOCORRO *enters carrying an envelope.*
SOCORRO: Well, it's another letter from Lia.
PEDRO: *(Looking up)* The consulate dropped it off?
SOCORRO: Yes, sweetheart.
PEDRO: It still makes me uncomfortable.
SOCORRO: What does?
PEDRO: Her sending things by diplomatic courier to us. And these so-called "revolutionary" officials showing up at our home with envelopes and packages. *(Putting the newspaper down and standing up)* Why can't she use regular air mail?
SOCORRO: *(Giving him a look)* With all the problems in Cuba today? *(Opening the envelop)* I don't think regular mail service has been restored since—
PEDRO: *(Rolling his eyes)*—Fidel's "revolution."
SOCORRO: *Alejandro's.*
PEDRO: It's Fidel Castro.
SOCORRO: Please drop it. *(Pause)* It's not our country. It's not our place to criticize what the Cuban people are doing or are not doing—and, besides, if Lía is happy there, who are we to say anything?
PEDRO: Well, I don't like it. *(Walking over to* SOCORRO*)* What does she say?
SOCORRO: *(Putting on her reading glasses, she unfolds the letter, and reads)* "My dearest Mother and Father. I pray the good Lord has kept you safe since my last

letter. There are no words to describe the exuberance I feel about the future and how happy I am in Cuba. For the first time in my life I feel completely alive! I don't know what is being said about the Cuban Revolution in the international press, but I can tell you that I am living this Great Revolution every single day! All the Revolutionaries were thrilled with the marvelous propaganda Herbert Matthews published in the *New York Times*, and it has helped galvanize volunteers from the world over to come to Cuba, join the Revolution, and enlist in the Literacy Brigades. Back home, I was a teacher to one classroom of children. But here, I am a teacher to an entire country. Alejandro is still the dream he was when I first met him; he makes my heart skip a beat and his sincere love for Cuba is astounding! Che says that true Revolution is guided by a great feeling of love. And he is right! And the Cuban people love him! The truth is that the public adores all the revolutionaries. If only one day we Mexicans had leaders we respected and adored! If only one day Mexico had leaders who loved Mexico more than they love their bank accounts! I know that you, Father, do not approve of my being in a foreign country, but let me assure you: I am respected, I am valued, and I am truly contributing in my own way to the betterment of this great country. I miss the both of you—and my beloved sister—and I hope you will come to Havana soon. Alejandro has ordered the Consulate in Mérida to make all arrangements for you to come to Cuba whenever you want. Until then, Mother, please, please, please send chocolates. That's all I ask. Alejandro adores them. With all the love in the world, yours in Revolution, Lía."

PEDRO: See?

SOCORRO: See what?

PEDRO: She still calls him Alejandro, not Fidel!

SOCORRO: *(Giving him a look)* Drop it, I said! *(Looking up)* She sounds so happy.

PEDRO: Send the lovebirds chocolate? *(Pause)* How about

sending her a one-way ticket so she can come home!
SOCORRO: Pedro!
PEDRO: She sounds like a naïve teeny-bopper, if you ask me. The Beatles. Have you seen the girls these days? They're jumping up and down screaming over those long-haired British freaks! And their music, talk about noise! *(Raising his finger)* Now this, this is music!
SOCORRO: They are cute, aren't they?
PEDRO: Who?
SOCORRO: The Beatles?
PEDRO: The Beatles? Who cares about The Beatles?
SOCORRO: But you brought them up!
PEDRO: Yes, I did—but only in a dismissive manner! *(Irritated)* That's not proper music for decent girls. If young people keep listening to that kind of music, before you know it, kids all over the world will be carrying on like idiots.
SOCORRO: *(Rolling her eyes)* Whatever you say, sweetheart.
PEDRO: I didn't like the way you said that!
SOCORRO: Be happy that I'm still calling you sweetheart ... sweetheart!
PEDRO: Can't a man express his opinions about what's going on in pop culture—and in the world without being mocked?
SOCORRO: And what, exactly, is going on?
PEDRO: Are you blind? Can't you see?
SOCORRO: See what?
PEDRO: Out daughter is in a foreign country that is taking actions against the United States! The United States of America!
SOCORRO: Weren't you the one desperate to get her to stop teaching the Maya so-called "peasants"?
PEDRO: Yes, but I didn't mean for her to go to distant towns in *Cuba* and squander her times with *Cuban* peasants, for goodness sake! I just wanted her to stay here in Mérida where she was more likely to find a—
SOCORRO: —find a what?
PEDRO: A suitable young man to marry—and not spending

her time in small towns filled with peasants.
SOCORRO: Peasants?
PEDRO: *(Ignoring her comment)* First, she's out there in indigenous villages teaching peasants, and now *(making the sign of the cross)* she's carrying on with Cuban revolutionary crazies!
SOCORRO: Crazies?
PEDRO: Yes, crazies.
SOCORRO: *(Adamant)* What do you mean?
PEDRO: What do you mean, what do I mean?
SOCORRO: Explain yourself.
PEDRO: Explain what?
SOCORRO: You just made a statement—and I want you to defend it.
PEDRO: Alright. *(Pause)* That those so-called revolutionaries in Cuba are crazy.
SOCORRO: Crazy?
PEDRO: They are crazy to provoke the United States—which is a country filled with even more crazies than Cuba!
SOCORRO: And what's so crazy about the Americans?
PEDRO: One word: Miami!
SOCORRO: Miami?
PEDRO: The Woolworth counter? The racist laws on who sits where on a public bus or at a diner counter or even walking down the street?
SOCORRO: Oh, alright. *(Looking at him with a mischievous grin)* You win. The Americans are an unhinged people.
PEDRO: And Cuba is becoming a mirror image of … unhingedness …
SOCORRO: Unhingedness? *(With a smirk)* That's not even a word.
PEDRO: I happen to think it is.
SOCORRO: Well, it isn't!
PEDRO: If it isn't, it should be.
SOCORRO: It's not a word, I tell you!
PEDRO: Well, if our daughter, the teacher, were here, she could settle the matter! But she isn't! And she isn't because she's running around in a tropical socialist

paradise that—at any moment—will see an American invasion!

SOCORRO: *(Surprised)* An invasion? Why do you say that?

PEDRO: Because that's what the Americans do, invade and occupy countries. I have no doubt that if things continue as they are, the Americans will invade Cuba.

SOCORRO: *(Somberly)* That's not very hopeful.

PEDRO: What does hope have to do with it? *(Pause)* I'm being realistic. And I'm concerned for our daughter—as you should also be.

SOCORRO: Why?

PEDRO: Because she's in a dangerous situation, Socorro.

SOCORRO: Dangerous?

PEDRO: Don't you hear the news? *(Walking to pick up the newspaper)* Every day planes arrive at our airport and Cubans—people who have been exiled—get off. *(Handing her the newspaper)* There are thousands of Cubans who have been thrown out of their country all over town. Some are staying and some are going to Mexico City. Those who have connections in Europe are going to Spain. *(Pause)* But the vast majority are going to Miami—that bastion of American insanity. *(Slowly)* It's not a happy revolution, Socorro. No matter what Lía writes in her letters to us.

SOCORRO: Is it really that bad?

PEDRO: It's the French Revolution all over again.

SOCORRO: What?

PEDRO: It's like that French journalist, Jacques Mallet du Pan—

SOCORRO: —who?

PEDRO: He's the eighteenth century French writer! Remember? He said, "The Revolution devours its children."

SOCORRO: And?

PEDRO: And that's happening in Cuba right now.

SOCORRO: It is?

PEDRO: Of course. *(Pausing, looking pensive)* Who was that hero of the Cuban Revolution who disappeared?

SOCORRO: —which one?

PEDRO: The one Lía thought was a wonderful man when she met him at the airport when she arrived in Havana. *(Pause)* He's the one whose plane just vanished out of the sky.

SOCORRO: Camilo Cienfuegos.

PEDRO: Yes, that's the one. *(Pointedly)* Well, do you really think his plane just disappeared? It isn't as if it flew into the Bermuda Triangle, right?

SOCORRO: Then what happened?

PEDRO: I don't know what happened, but what I can say is that Camilo Cienfuegos' death was very, very convenient for the Castro brothers!

SOCORRO: *(Gasping)* Are you suggesting foul play? Planes do disappear once in a while?

PEDRO: Do they?

SOCORRO: Amelia Earhart disappeared—and no one knows what happened to her!

PEDRO: That's different?

SOCORRO: How?

PEDRO: Amelia Earhart's plane disappeared over the waters of an open ocean! But Camilo Cienfuegos' plane just vanished without a trace on a short flight back to Havana!

SOCORRO: Was he killed?

PEDRO: Why should the Cuban Revolution be the exception to the rule that all revolutions devour their children?

SOCORRO: *(Alarmed)* But Alejandro—I mean, Fidel—was such a polite young man.

PEDRO: Not any more, Socorro. *(Pause)* And the situation in Cuba's getting worse.

SOCORRO: How?

PEDRO: Do you remember that Spanish-style building in downtown Miami when you were there with the girls?

SOCORRO: Which one?

PEDRO: The offices of *The Miami News* newspaper.

SOCORRO: Yes. *(Pause)* The one with the beautiful Spanish cupola. What of it?

PEDRO: The newspaper moved out and the building is now being used to process Cuban refugees.

SOCORRO: Refugees?

PEDRO: Yes, refugees. The "Freedom Tower" they're calling it.

SOCORRO: Freedom Tower?

PEDRO: *(Raising his eyebrows)* What's happening in Cuba is without precedent in the Americas, honey.

SOCORRO: *(Concerned)* What do you mean? Without precedent?

PEDRO: What I mean is that it's become a humanitarian crisis. It's a social upheaval unlike anything that's ever happened in our hemisphere—apart from the social crisis in the U.S. during the American Civil War in the nineteenth century—and the political upheavals during our own Mexican Revolution half a century ago.

SOCORRO: *(Concerned)* Do you think Lía is safe?

PEDRO: *(With apprehension)* I am sure she is for now, but I don't know what will happen when the Americans strike back.

SOCORRO: Strike back? Do you think they are going to support an overthrow?

PEDRO: I don't know. *(Pause)* But I wouldn't be surprised, since the Americans overthrow governments the world over all the time. *(Pause)* But I do know she doesn't really know what's going on.

SOCORRO: How do you know that?

PEDRO: I just do.

SOCORRO: *(Challenging)* Do you think you have a better understanding of what's going on than she does, considering she's there?

PEDRO: *(Putting his hand on her shoulder)* Well, here we are, fretting about what's going in Cuba, and all she wants is for you to send her chocolates!

SOCORRO: *(Laughing)* That is funny, really.

PEDRO: It isn't funny to me!

SOCORRO: You're just getting all worked up over nothing!

PEDRO: Am I?

SOCORRO: Yes, you are!

PEDRO: Well, I just wish things were a bit more ...

SOCORRO: More what?

PEDRO: *(Bashful)* Matriarchal.

SOCORRO: What?

PEDRO: You heard me!

SOCORRO: I don't think I did! *(Pause)* What did you say?

PEDRO: I said "matriarchal."

SOCORRO: Matriarchal?

PEDRO: It's a word! You can't argue that *that* isn't a word! M-A-T-R-I-A-C-H-A-L.

SOCORRO: Have you been reading *National Geographic* again?

PEDRO: What of it? It's a good magazine!

SOCORRO: *(With skepticism)* And what does matriarchy have anything to do with the Cuban Revolution, may I ask?

PEDRO: Everything.

SOCORRO: Is that so?

PEDRO: Yes, Socorro. In a patriarchal society, the sons leave the family, take on wives, and form their own households. But in a matriarchal society, the daughters stay home, and when they marry, it is their husbands that go live with their wives' families.

SOCORRO: What?

PEDRO: It's not that difficult! We have two daughters, so they're going to go off with the men they married and form their own families—but if this were a matriarchal society, then they'd be close to home because their husbands would move in!

SOCORRO: And if we had two sons?

PEDRO: Then I wouldn't care, since sons go off and do what they want. Truth be told, if we had two sons, I'd be glad they were on their own.

SOCORRO: Really?

PEDRO: Well, of course! *(Adamant)* Everyone knows that sons are more needy that daughters.

SOCORRO: Well, I'm glad you admit it!

PEDRO: It's true! *(Pause)* Daughters can handle life; sons are wimps. Daughter can take it, but sons, well, grown men are more likely to faint at the sight of a drop of blood than women. Men are wimps.
SOCORRO: Then what you're saying is that Lía can take care of herself in Cuba?
PEDRO: That's not it at all!
SOCORRO: That's what it sounds like to me!
PEDRO: What I meant to say is that, if we lived in a matriarchal society, instead of Lía going to Cuba, Fidel would come here!
SOCORRO: Come here?
PEDRO: That's how matriarchal societies work!
SOCORRO: But he's the Prime Minister of Cuba!
PEDRO: Well, who says he can't be the Prime Minister of Cuba from Mérida?
SOCORRO: What?
PEDRO: There are telephones! There are telegraphs! There are airplanes! He can govern Cuba from Mexico, right?
SOCORRO: I don't think that's how it works.
PEDRO: Well, it should work that way. *(Pause)* I mean, why should he take our baby girl away, just because he's busy running—or ruining—a country?
SOCORRO: *(With sympathetic)* I miss her too, Pedro. I really do.
PEDRO: Can you blame me for trying to figure out a way of getting her back home?
SOCORRO: *(Softly)* No, no one can blame a father for missing his daughter.
PEDRO: I just don't know, Socorro. *(Pause)* I've been losing sleep over her being in Cuba.
SOCORRO: And I also worry about the changes taking place on that beautiful island. *(Pause)* Lía reassures us everything is wonderful, but the news out of Cuba, as you point out, is scary.
The husband and wife look at each other.
PEDRO: Well, let's go.
SOCORRO: Let's go where?

PEDRO: The chocolate shop. Isn't that what she asked for? Chocolates? Then that's what we'll get her, chocolates!

SOCORRO: The chocolate shop?

PEDRO: Don't we have to buy chocolates to send her? *(Surprised)* Our baby girl is in Cuba and desperate for authentic chocolates!

SOCORRO: She remembers the flavors of home.

PEDRO: I *know* she misses home—I'm *sure* she's homesick!

Scene 6

Santa Isabel de las Lajas, Cienfuegos Province, Cuba. 1961

A schoolroom. Cuban flags are draped on the doors and a framed photograph of Fidel Castro hangs on the wall. There is a chalkboard against the wall and about a classroom of adult students; she speaks in the direction of the audience, as if they were part of the classroom. There are four words written in chalk on the chalkboard: "Socratic Method/Método Socrático." LÍA CÁMARA *stands at the front of the class and is speaking to the students.*

LÍA: Reading and writing are skills that let us to understand others and let others to understand us. We know what was in José Martí's mind and heart because he wrote his thoughts and feelings down on paper. And because *we* can read, we can read *his* words—these many years later—and understand the love and passion he felt for Cuba. And, now that *you* can read and write, *you* will be able to write down *your* thoughts and feelings. And when you do that, others—even those not yet born—will be able to read what was in your mind and your heart.

LÍA *moves to the chalkboard, picks up a ruler and turns to the class.*

LÍA: The Revolution has bestowed upon you the gift of the alphabet, as I am fond of saying. And with that alphabet, you have learned how to make words, string those words together, and compose sentences. With that alphabet you have learned how to read the sentences—and poems—others have written. And *now,* the Revolution's greatest gift of all: how ... to ... *think* ...

CHE *appears at the door. The students are unaware of his presence. He listens attentively as she continues to teach.*

LÍA: How do we think? *(Pause)* How do we, as humans, make

sense of the world, interpret the world, understand our experience, and then come to conclusions about the world in which we live? More importantly, how can thinking helps us distinguish between what is true and what is false?

She looks at the students, pausing for a moment, allowing her words to sink in. She picks up a ruler and points to the chalkboard.

LÍA: Socrates. Who remembers Socrates from last week's class? *(She sees a few hands go up)* Good! Socrates, as we began to discuss, was a Greek philosopher who was one of the founders of Western philosophy. He was one of the first thinkers who *thought* about *thinking*, thought about how to determine what is true, and gave us a process that helps us arrive at what is true by identifying what is false.

She underlines "Socratic Method" in chalk.

LÍA: Who remembers our discussions about the Socratic Method? *(Again, she sees a few hands go up)* Good! I'm glad something is sticking! *(A few students laugh)* The Socratic Method is a dialectical way of arriving at the truth. It is a conversation in the form of an argumentative dialogue between individuals, cooperative discussions among debaters. The purpose of which is to ask and answer questions in a simulation of critical thinking in order to understand the ideas and underlying presumptions of a claim. The key to the Socratic Method is critical thinking!

CHE *begins to clap his hands in a loud and mocking manner.* LÍA *notices him for the first time.*

CHE: Bravo, Maestra Lía! *(Walking to the front of the class)* Bravo, bravo, bravo. *(Turning to, and addressing, the class)* What a fine class of students! A few months ago almost none of you could even write your own name—and now—thanks to this exceptional teacher—you are . . . learning criticism, *critical thinking*, and the Socratic Method!

LÍA *smiles proudly.* CHE *turns to her, and claps. Then,*

abruptly, the smile vanishes from his face. A guard—the one that appeared in the first scene of Act I—appears at the door, unnoticed. This time he sports a beard and is wearing the green uniform of the revolutionaries.

CHE: *(To* LÍA*)* A wonderful job you have done, Maestra Lía. *(To the students)* Raise your hand in you believe in the Socratic Method. *(Half a dozen students raise their hands;* CHE *nods in approval)* Very, very impressive! A class of eager and capable students! *(To* LÍA*)* I congratulate you, Maestra Lía, on instructing the men and women that will make this Revolution the envy of the world.

LÍA: Thank you, Che.

CHE'S *smile vanishes and he moves closer, invading her personal space. She steps back and he takes the ruler she is holding.*

CHE: *(To* LÍA*)* What is your understanding of the Socratic Method?

LÍA: *(Hiding her apprehension)* I was not prepared for a pop quiz!

CHE *steps back; a few students laugh.*

CHE: *(To* LÍA*)* Go on. *(Pause, mockingly)* Answer me, wise teacher.

LÍA: *(With confidence)* The Socratic Method is a way of eliminating hypotheses.

Che: *(To* LÍA*)* How?

LÍA: *(With confidence)* Well, the process of elimination takes place when better hypotheses are found through the process of identifying and eliminating those that lead to contradictions.

CHE: *(Turning to the class)* That's right, but that was then. It is no longer true! *(To* LÍA*)* Socrates lived thousands of years ago and since then we have advanced much, *(sarcastically)* my dear, precious Maestra Lía.

LÍA: *(Pointedly)* Truth is eternal.

CHE: (CHE *puts down the ruler, walks to the chalkboard, and begins to erase "Socratic Method/Método Socrático" and instead writes "Karl Marx/Friedrich Engels." He speaks the following as he writes on the chalkboard)* Humanity has learned much since the times of Socrates. In fact, Karl Marx and Friedrich Engels solved the *problem* of history—and we are the beneficiaries of their thinking. *(Turning to the class)* The Socratic Method *ended* when Marx and Engels *solved* history. *(To* LÍA*)* Isn't that the case?

LÍA: *(Pointedly)* Solved history? History never ends.

CHE: *(To* LÍA, *forcefully)* It! Just! Has! (Ignoring her, addressing the students directly) Class, one more lesson for today. The thesis is an intellectual proposition. It is then challenged by the antithesis, a critical perspective on the thesis. And then the conflict is resolved through the synthesis, which ends the contradiction between the thesis and antithesis through the reconciliation of their common truths, thus forming a new proposition.

LÍA: *(Pointedly)* Which then becomes the new thesis, to be challenged by another synthesis. And so on.

CHE: *(To* LÍA*)* Enough school for one day! *(Addressing the students)* Could those who raised their hands because they believe in the Socratic Method stand? *(He addresses the students who raise their hands)* Very good, very good! I want all of you to go with the guard. *(We hear the sounds of students picking up their books and walk to the* GUARD, *who exits)* Class is over for the day. The rest of you are dismissed. *(We hear more sounds of students picking up their books and exiting, leaving* CHE *and* LÍA *alone)* Now, let's go over the lesson plan *(mockingly)* Maestra Lía.

LÍA: Why should I answer to you?

CHE: You do answer to me.

LÍA: Well, I'm responsible for the lesson plans—and I have authority to develop them at my discretion.

CHE: You have the final word over the lesson plans?

LÍA: Yes, I have ownership of the lesson plans, Che.

CHE: That kind of "ownership" is very bourgeois in its thinking, my very bourgeois citizen of a very bourgeois Mexico. *(Pause. Pointedly)* Don't you get it?

LÍA: Get what?
CHE: That the proletariat needs to be *told* what it *wants*.
LÍA: Proletariat?
CHE: Yes, proletariat.
LÍA: The "proletariat," as you call the Cubans, are people and people are comprised of individuals—
CHE: —what?
LÍA: —And individuals have names.
CHE: *(As he moves around her, invading her personal space)* And those individuals—with names or without names— are the *masses* and the *masses* are the *proletariat!*
LÍA: That's one opinion—
CHE: *(Raised voice)* That's the *only* opinion that counts!
LÍA: You're wrong!
CHE: What's the matter with you?
LÍA: The matter with me?
CHE: You stupid—*(with condescension)*—woman.
LÍA: How dare you!
CHE: The proletariat has to be told what it wants so the goal of Greater Socialism can be achieved.
LÍA: You can't force people to think what you want them to think.
CHE: Watch me!
LÍA: What?
CHE: The Revolution is not an apple that falls when it is ripe. You have to make it fall.
LÍA: That's not what the Literacy Brigades are about, brainwashing people into thinking what you want them to think.
CHE *reaches for a pocket and takes out a piece of paper. He holds it up.*
CHE: Yes, literacy is important—crucial to the Revolution. *(Pause)* We want everyone to read, yes. We want everyone to write, yes. But we—the Revolutionary Government—will tell them *what* to read and *what* to write.
LÍA: That can't be!
CHE: Why not? Why can't it be? Haven't we risked our lives

and struggled for years to rule as we think best?
LÍA: No, you haven't.
CHE: *(Reaching for the paper)* The only independent thinking we want is for every Cuban to come to the conclusion that Fidel is the one who knows the Final Truth.
LÍA: And what is the Final Truth?
CHE: I'll read it for you, Maestra: "When, in the course of development, class distinctions have disappeared, and all production has been concentrated in the hands of a vast association of the whole nation, the public power will lose its political character. Political power, properly so called, is merely the organized power of one class for oppressing another. If the proletariat during its contest with the bourgeoisie is compelled, by the force of circumstances, to organize itself as a class; if, by means of a revolution, it makes itself the ruling class, and, as such, sweeps away by force the old conditions of production, then it will, along with these conditions, have swept away the conditions for the existence of class antagonisms and of classes generally, and will thereby have abolished its own supremacy as a class. In place of the old bourgeois society, with its classes and class antagonisms, we shall have an association in which the free development of each is the condition for the free development of all."
LÍA: You quote from *The Communist Manifesto*, as if that were beyond debate.
CHE: Section II, "Proletarians and Communists."
LÍA: *(With pride, pushing back)* You're guilty of conjunction fallacy.
CHE: What's that?
LÍA: Ask Marx.
CHE: You will find that there are bourgeois dreams that the proletariat's reality will kill.
An uneasy silence falls between them as they stare at each other. Suddenly, we hear gunfire, startling LÍA, *who jumps.* CHE, *coolly lights a cigar and puffs on it,*

smiling with satisfaction at her unease.

LÍA: What was that?

CHE: *Paredón. (Blowing cigar smoke, mocking,)* Revolutionary justice.

LÍA: *(Horrified)* What?

CHE: The firing squad. *(Mocking)* Socrates is long dead—and so are those who believe in his method.

LÍA *rushes to the door, stands in the doorway, screams, and covers her face.* CHE *lights a cigar.* LÍA *turns around, her anger turns to resolve. She looks defiantly at* CHE.

LÍA: *(Stepping back in horror, her voice quivering)* You had them shot?

CHE: Of course.

LÍA: Why?

CHE: Because we must purge society of the feeble-minded, of those who sympathize with capitalists, and of the vulnerable who can be manipulated by the bourgeois.

LÍA: *(With backbone, enraged)* You are evil!

CHE: (CHE *walks slowly to her and takes her by both wrists; she resists. Then, slowly and with arrogance)* What did you say, you stupid, bourgeois wretch?

LÍA *breaks free and stands back.*

LÍA: You had them shot because they *learned* what I *taught* them!

CHE: Then modify your lesson plans! *(Seething with jealousy)* The only thing that spares *your* life is that you're the future First Lady of Cuba. *(*LÍA *moves away, fearful)* What? Suddenly this know-it-all teacher has nothing to say! Isn't that something? The cat got your tongue?

LÍA: It wouldn't be your cat, Che. Your cats are all drowned.

CHE: *(Laughing)* And so they are!

LÍA *stands turns away;* CHE *moves to her, hovering over her in an intimidating manner.*

LÍA: I have nothing to say to you.

CHE: Yes you do, but you won't. *(Pause, then with a dramatic delivery)* Silence is argument carried out by other means.

Scene 7

Havana, Cuba. 1961

The Mexican Embassy in Havana. Ambassador GILBERTO BOQUES *is at his desk. There is the seal of the Mexican Republic and a Mexican flag decorating the office. There are stacks of folders on his desk and a telephone. He sits at his desk.* RAÚL CASTRO *is seating across from him. The men are conversing while enjoying afternoon tea.*

RAÚL: It's always good to see you, Ambassador. I don't have to remind you of the great admiration and respect we have for Mexico.

BOSQUES: Mexico is a friend of Cuba and we want your new government to be successful.

RAÚL: *(Slowly, playing with the handle on his tea cup)* Yes, of course. *(The men stare at each other, uneasily)* Our Revolution needs friends, friends who understand—the—who understand the—

BOSQUES:—process?

RAÚL: Yes, that's the precise word. Process. The *process* of *change.*

BOSQUES: I see.

RAÚL: *(Eagerly)* Do you? Do you see?

BOSQUES: During our own Revolution half a century ago, we embarked on radical reforms—reforms which were frowned upon by—

RAÚL:—the United States.

BOSQUES: I think the Americans are still angry at Mexico for our nationalizing the oil industry—a quarter century ago.

RAÚL: But they didn't intervene, did they?

BOSQUES: No, they didn't, but we didn't know whether or not they would. Fortunately, FDR understood that each country has to find its own solutions that are appropriate for its own people. *(Pouring* RAÚL *tea)* But the course that Cuba's leadership has embarked upon is raising eyebrows.

RAÚL: The nationalizations?

BOSQUES: There is concern that the properties of Mexican citizens are being seized, yes. And there is concern that the civil rights of Mexicans living in Cuba are at risk, yes.

RAÚL: *(Smiling)* Our policies are not aimed at Mexican citizens, you understand.

BOSQUES: I am aware of that. *(Pause)* I know your government is taking specific actions against specific economic classes—

RAÚL:—and not nationalities.

BOSQUES: The bourgeois, correct? *(Pause, smiling)* That's your Revolution's enemy, the bourgeois.

RAÚL: The proletariat is now in control—through the Revolutionary government.

BOSQUES: Of course. *(Pause)* As I have mentioned, my government has expressed reservations over Cuba's turn to Communism as an economic model, but we respect Cuban sovereignty. And we will remain a friend to Cuba without question.

RAÚL: I thank you for that. Especially since the United States is attempting to isolate us, turning our friends and neighbors against us.

BOSQUES: Let me reassure you that even if the United States is successful in having the Organization of American States suspend Cuba's membership, Mexico will not, under any circumstances, sever diplomatic relations with your government.

RAÚL: Fidel will be glad to know that.

BOSQUES: Of course.

RAÚL *stands and slowly paces around the room, carrying the teacup and saucer.* BOSQUES *watches* RAÚL *carefully.*

RAÚL: Now, there's a different matter. *(Pause, sipping tea)* There is an unexplained occurrence taking place at the airport.

BOSQUES: Which is?

RAÚL: It appears that the number of Mexicans departing Havana is larger than the number of Mexicans arriving in Cuba.

BOSQUES: Oh?

RAÚL: Mexicana Airlines has a daily flight that originates in Mexico City, stops at Mérida, and continues to Havana where the flight terminates. Two hours later, the plane returns to Mérida before continuing on to Mexico City where that flight terminates. *(There is a pause as he pours himself more tea)* The flights arrive two-thirds empty and depart completely full. *(Staring at the* BOSQUES*)* Don't you find it odd that more Mexicans are leaving Cuba than are arriving?

BOSQUES: More Mexicans are leaving Cuba than are arriving in Cuba?

RAÚL: Yes, isn't that odd?

BOSQUES: *(Smiling)* The explanation I can offer is to speculate that perhaps there are many Mexicans living in Cuba as permanent residents who are now returning to Mexico because of the change of government.

RAÚL: Could that be it?

BOSQUES: I believe that is the case. Many Mexicans believe darkness has fallen over Cuba.

RAÚL *laughs.*

RAÚL: Darkness? On the contrary: Light shines like never before.

BOSQUES: Light can blind at times.

RAÚL: *(Putting down his teacup and saucer)* Very well, then, perhaps there is an exodus of bourgeois Mexicans leaving Cuba. We will look into it. *(Turning to leave)* For now, I will tell Fidel that, no matter what the American Imperialists do, we can count on Mexico's friendship.

Scene 8

Havana, Cuba. 1961

An office in the Vedado district of Havana. It is an ample office with two desks, several cabinets, and chairs. There are documents stacked all over the place. There is now a large portrait of nineteenth century German philosopher Karl Marx on the wall. There is also a large hammer and sickle mounted on the wall. FIDEL CASTRO *sits at his desk.* LÍA CÁMARA *walks in and closes the door behind her.*

LÍA: I have to talk to you.
FIDEL: *(Standing up)* Very well, speak up.
LÍA: What's going on?
FIDEL: What do you mean?
LÍA: I had a confrontation with Che about the Literacy Campaign.
FIDEL: I know. He told me.
LÍA: He told you?
FIDEL: Yes. He told me.
LÍA: I see.
FIDEL: Do you? *(Pause, as he moves closer to her)* Tell me, honestly, what do you think of Che?
LÍA: What do I think of him?
FIDEL: Yes, it's a simple question, Lía.
LÍA: *(She pauses, hesitating, then slowly speaks up)* I think Che is …
FIDEL: Is what?
LÍA: *(With confidence)* I think Che is a sadist.
FIDEL: *(Smiling, taking her by the hand)* I remember standing in your parents' home and asking you that I always wanted you to speak the truth to me, no matter what. Do you remember that?
LÍA: Yes.
FIDEL: Then why are you lying to me now?

LÍA: *(Surprised and defensive)* Lying? But I'm not lying! I think Che is a sadist.
FIDEL: No, Lía. You don't think Che is a sadist.
LÍA: How do you know?
FIDEL: Because I know you think Che is a sociopath.
LÍA: *(Stepping back)* Then why?
FIDEL: Then why what?
LÍA: Then why do you have him around? I didn't want to call him a sociopath—
FIDEL: —that's what he is.
LÍA: Then why?
FIDEL: He's handsome. The ladies love him. He's a great poster boy for the Revolution. And Raúl is fond of him. Sometimes too much so.
LÍA: But if you know he's a sociopath, why have him around at all? He's dangerous.
FIDEL: He's not dangerous. *(Pause)* He's a useful idiot, Lía. And he's useful to me—and my Revolution.
LÍA: Useful to *your* Revolution?
FIDEL: Lía, I *am* the Revolution.
LÍA: And your Revolution needs a sociopath on its side? *(Pause)* Do you think you can control a sociopath?
FIDEL: Yes. I can control anyone.
LÍA: What if you can't?
FIDEL: Then, so what? *(Pause)* The world is filled with tragic martyrs useful idiots can worship. When the time comes and he's no longer useful, I'll get rid of him.
LÍA: The way you're getting rid of so many—
FIDEL: —bourgeois counter-revolutionaries?
LÍA: I was going to say compatriots.
FIDEL: What you call compatriots are scum, capitalist maggots and worms that cling to the past, a past based on the exploitation of our fellow human beings.
LÍA: Do you really believe that?
FIDEL: I believe that history pulls us to one, single truth. I believe history has led us to this one inescapable didactic path to the future.
LÍA: Marxism.

FIDEL: Yes. Marxism.

LÍA: And where are we now?

FIDEL: Now?

LÍA: Well, along your so-called inescapable path to your one, single truth.

FIDEL: *(Smiling)* As a student of history, then you know the Revolution must consolidate itself through the establishment of the Dictatorship of the Proletariat.

LÍA: Dictatorship?

FIDEL: Of the proletariat. *(Pause)* That's where we are at *this moment in time*: the Dictatorship of the Proletariat.

LÍA *moves away. They stare at each other.*

LÍA: *(Sternly)* I don't recognize you any longer, Alejandro.

FIDEL: *(Angered)* It's Fidel. My name is Fidel and I am Cuba.

LÍA: No, you're not.

FIDEL: *(In a loud voice)* YES I AM! I AM CUBA! I AM THE CUBAN STATE!

LÍA: No, you're not—because you can't be! *(Mockingly)* Have you forgotten what Marx boasted?

FIDEL: *(As if to challenge)* What was that?

LÍA: That it all ends with the withering away of the state.

FIDEL: What?

LÍA: If *you* are the Cuban State, then it all ends when you, a forgotten old man, wither away.

FIDEL: *(He grabs her wrist and pulls her close)* You will accept my marriage proposal. You will be my First Lady. And you will be joyful being my wife and Cuba's First Lady.

LÍA: Joyful?

FIDEL: *This* Revolution is *joyful!*

LÍA: Unhand me! *(Pulling free)* I am not your property—because under Communism, there is no such thing as property!

FIDEL: *(In a loud voice)* You are mine!

LÍA: *(Defiantly)* No, Alejandro, I'm not.

FIDEL: *(In a raised voice)* My name if Fidel!

LÍA: *(Coldly)* Have you forgotten what my father taught you?

FIDEL: *(Sarcastically)* Your old man wanted to teach me

much.

LÍA: Alejandro would remember what my Father taught him. I'm not sure if Fidel cares to remember an older generation's wisdom.

FIDEL: Don't anger me.

LÍA: Would the truth *anger* you?

FIDEL: What truth?

LÍA: Let me remind you. *(Pause, as he nears hers)* Intelligence, in excess, leads to insanity.

FIDEL *grabs her wrist; she resists, frees herself and slaps him across the face.*

FIDEL: *(Yelling)* No one on *this* island can deny *me* anything!

Moving quickly to the door. She turns around, looks at him. They stare at each other.

LÍA: You're not the man I fell in love with, Alejandro. You've become the "monstruo" José Martí warned us all about!

FIDEL: *(Enraged)* How dare you speak to me this way!

LÍA: *(With sadness)* Where is the Alejandro I knew, the Alejandro who strolled down the streets of my hometown and spoke of good things? Where is the Alejandro who saw the world through benevolent eyes? Where's the Alejandro whose photograph I have framed in my home and in my heart?

FIDEL: *(Enraged)* Don't you see that we have to be forceful in removing the Imperialist cancer that threatens the Cuban nation? Don't you see the great things we are doing—great things that will cast away whatever doubts you might have?

LÍA: *(Turning away from Fidel Castro)* No, Alejandro. A million times no.

FIDEL: *(Enraged)* How dare you? How dare speak to me this way!

LÍA: You've become a madman.

FIDEL: I am still Fidel!

LÍA: I only know Alejandro, not Fidel!

FIDEL: *(Yelling)* Where are you going?

LÍA: I have lesson plans to prepare.

FIDEL: *(Yelling)* I have not dismissed you!
LÍA: *(Whispering)* Adios, Alejandro.
LÍA *exits, closing the door behind her.*
FIDEL: *(With deliberation, yelling in rage)* No one denies me anything!

Scene 9

Havana, Cuba. 1961

The Mexican Embassy in Havana. Ambassador GILBERTO BOQUES *is at his desk. The intercom buzzes and he answers.*

BOSQUES: Yes, please ask her to come in.
He hangs up and closes an open file on his desk. The door opens and LÍA *enters.* BOSQUES *stands to meet her.*
LÍA: *(Shaking his extended hand)* Thank you for seeing me, Mr. Ambassador.
BOSQUES: Would you like some tea, Ms. Cámara.
LÍA: No thank you, Mr. Ambassador. *(Pause, then quickly blurting out)* I'm in danger.
BOSQUES: *(Walking back to his desk, he speaks softly)* Danger? What do you mean?
LÍA: *(Pleading)* I fear for my life.
BOSQUES: *(Calmly)* Are you sure you don't care for tea? It would calm your nerves. A very civilized custom, drinking tea in the afternoon.
LÍA: What? *(Pause)* No, no. *(With urgency)* Do you understand what I'm saying?
BOSQUES: *(Turning to her and speaking with conviction bordering on anger)* Ms. Cámara, I am aware of your situation at present. *(Pause, his anger subsiding and in an avuncular manner)* Do you think we don't know who you are? Do you think we dismiss you as an ordinary Mexican tourist on holiday in revolutionary Havana?
LÍA: *(Stepping back, taken aback)* You know who I am?
BOSQUES: *(With deliberation)* You may be a young woman, but you can't possibly be that naïve. *(Pause)* Yes, giving political speeches on behalf of the revolutionary government from balconies overlooking public plazas all over Cuba is not the best way to keep a low profile, is it?
LÍA: Yes, I have spoken at rallies with Che at my side.

BOSQUES: Among some of the other misguided revolutionaries unleashed upon this doomed island.

LÍA: Then you know I am privy to confidential things.

BOSQUES: A Mexican citizen who has access to Fidel Castro's innermost circle has raised eyebrows. Not just in Mexico City. And not just from Mexican intelligence.

LÍA: Then you know.

BOSQUES: Know what?

LÍA: Know that I'm in danger.

BOSQUES: And are you?

LÍA: Yes. *(With alarm)* Yes I am!

BOSQUES: And who is threatening you? Your groom-to-be?

LÍA: You know?

BOSQUES: Ms. Cámara, yes, I know. Mexican intelligence knows. The CIA knows.

LÍA: *(Surprised)* The CIA?

BOSQUES: There are only two things that are not known about you.

LÍA: What?

BOSQUES: Mexican intelligence would like to know if you're a Communist—not that they care, but they're just curious. And the CIA—

LÍA:—what do they want to know?

BOSQUES: The CIA would like know if you're willing to help assassinate Mr. Castro.

LÍA: *(Shocked)* What?

BOSQUES: That's Washington's new foreign policy towards Revolutionary Cuba. *(Pause)* The CIA has been watching you and they're interested in you only if you're willing to become a Mexican Mata Hari.

LÍA: *(Slowly)* If I've been spied on, then you know that I'm in danger. You know that I have to get out of here as soon as I can.

BOSQUES: Yes, you are correct. *(Looking at her intensely)* You are in danger.

LÍA: Then help me, please!

BOSQUES: I was wondering when you'd show up and ask for my help, young lady. *(In an avuncular fashion, with genuine concern)* I am not entirely unsympathetic to your situation. And I can understand your reluctance to continue your involvement in a government that, shall we say, is becoming more and more dogmatic in its philosophy with each passing execution.

LÍA: Fidel has surrounded himself with sociopaths.

BOSQUES: And how is the charming Che these days? I see he's graduated from drowning cats to sending Cubans to the firing squad.

LÍA: And Fidel is under his influence.

BOSQUES: And Raúl, that subtle beast with the temperamental smile, is even more smitten with Che. We know all about *that* as well. *(Pause)* Now, precisely what does Comandante Fidel want from you, Ms. Cámara?

LÍA: He wants something that—

BOSQUES: —you cannot countenance.

LÍA: That's the perfect word.

BOSQUES: It's understandable, your apprehension given these circumstances. *(Pause)* It would be rather extraordinary to have a Mexican citizen become the First Lady of Cuba, especially as Cuba embarks on this ill-conceived Communist experiment.

LÍA: He's no longer the man with whom I fell in love.

BOSQUES: Power changes people in most peculiar ways. What does your buddy, Che, say about power at his insipid rallies?

LÍA: He's not my "buddy;" he's a sociopath.

BOSQUES: Sociopaths, like everyone else, need buddies and you're his buddy whether you like it or not. *(Pause)* In any case, what did he say recently? Oh, yes: "Cruel leaders are replaced only to have new leaders turn cruel!"

LÍA: Yes, he said that.

BOSQUES: *(With a flourish of his hands)* And Fidel has proved Che prescient—with unintended irony. *(Pause)* Let me tell you about myself, so you understand how I've seen this all before. During the World War, I was stationed in France. And I had the privilege of helping people flee Hitler and Franco. And now, here in Cuba, I'm helping people flee the Communists. Fidel Castro is creating a Cuban Diaspora in Mexico and the United States, an extraordinary event that will have consequences for generations to come. *(Pause, smiling as he puts his hand on* LÍA'S *shoulder)* When this Revolution turned on its own people, it didn't occur to me that I would find myself helping a fellow Mexican flee Cuba.

LÍA: Then will you help me?

BOSQUES: Of course, Ms. Cámara. It is my duty and moral obligation to help you out of the predicament in which you find yourself. *(He motions for her to take a seat, as he walks around to sit in his chair)* When Fidel finds out you refuse to marry him, he will have you assassinated.

LÍA: That's my fear.

BOSQUES: And *his* greatest fear is that you will turn him down.

LÍA: Do you think he fears rejection?

BOSQUES: All tyrants fear their power will dissipate when the adulation ends.

LÍA: Do you believe that's true?

BOSQUES: Of course it is. *(Pause)* It *is* your intention to turn him down, isn't it?

LÍA: Yes, it is. *(Pleading)* All I want is to go home.

BOSQUES: Very well. *(Pause)* You are now under my protection.

LÍA: Thank you! *(Then calmly)* Thank you, Ms. Ambassador.

BOSQUES: You can thank me tomorrow.

LÍA: Thank you!

BOSQUES: *(Tapping his finger on the desk)* For now, I want you to go back to your office at the Literacy Brigades and act as if nothing has happened. You will work on your lesson plans and meet with Che, as scheduled.

LÍA: You know I'm meeting with him this evening?

BOSQUES: Courtesy of the CIA, yes.

LÍA: Good heavens. *(To herself)* How did this happen?
BOSQUES: How did what happen?
LÍA: This—this insane predicament.
BOSQUES: Love. A most ill-advised thing, especially among young people. *(All business)* Now, tomorrow afternoon, I want you to go have coffee at the Ambos Mundos Hotel in Old Havana at three o'clock. The rooftop terrace. You will be met by an official from the embassy. You will leave with him, and he will drive you to the airport, where I will be waiting for you.
LÍA: What if they find out?
BOSQUES: No need to fear; you are under my protection. *(Pause)* When you arrive at the airport, I will have a diplomatic passport for you, and the cover story is that you are going home to escort your sister to Havana.
LÍA: My sister?
BOSQUES: You don't know, then?
LÍA: Know what?
BOSQUES: Your sister made quite an impression on Raúl when he was in Mérida with Fidel.
LÍA: She did?
BOSQUES: Oh, yes. *(Pause, smiling)* As part of the Revolution's cultural triumph, your sister, an accomplished concert pianist, has an open invitation to come and perform in Havana.
LÍA: She has an open invitation?
BOSQUES: At Raúl's request, I might add. It seems the Castro brothers are enamored of the Cámara sisters.
LÍA: Tomorrow, after coffee at Ambos Mundos.
BOSQUES: At three o'clock. The rooftop terrace.
BOSQUES *stands and walks around to her.*
LÍA: *(As she stands)* I want to thank you so much, Mr. Ambassador.
BOSQUES: Ms. Cámara, I want you to know that you, through chance, have stumbled upon a great adventure—or misadventure—and you must be mindful of the grave implications of your involvement with Fidel.

LÍA: Yes, Mr. Ambassador, I know.

BOSQUES: Very well, I will take care of things for tomorrow. *(Pause)* Are you sure you don't want some tea? I'm going to ask my secretary to bring me some. A cup of tea for you, to settle your nerves?

LÍA: No, thank you, Mr. Ambassador. I'm too nervous.

BOSQUES: Very well, then. *(Pause)* One question.

LÍA: Yes, Mr. Ambassador.

BOSQUES: Do I have your permission to let our friends at the CIA know that you have no interest in participating in any of the assassination schemes the United States is contemplating?

LÍA: *(Shocked)* Oh, that's madness!

BOSQUES: Yes, there seems to be an epidemic of madness going around. On both sides of the Straits of Florida.

LÍA: *(Quietly, almost bashful)* I would never be part of any plot to harm him.

BOSQUES: Because you are a good Christian. *(Pause, smiling)* And as the good Christian that you are, you disapprove of political assassinations—especially in this case because ... you ... still ... *love* ... Fidel.

LÍA: *(Quietly, almost bashful)* Yes, I still love him.

BOSQUES: You still love a man who would order you killed if you left him. *(Slight pause, then smiling)* Makes sense to me.

LÍA: I don't know what to say.

BOSQUES: *(Escorting her to the door)* There's nothing to say, love is love and love is a form of madness. In fact, love is the kind of madness that lingers far longer than it should, defying all reason. *(Pause)* Tomorrow, at Ambos Mundos at three o'clock.

LÍA: Thank you, Mr. Ambassador. Thank you again.

LÍA *exits. He closes the door and walks back to his desk. He picks up a tape recorder microphone and then speaks.*

BOSQUES: *(Into the tape recorder)* Memo to file.

Scene 10

Havana, Cuba. 1961

An office in the Vedado district of Havana. There are now photographs of Vladimir Lenin and Mao Zedong prominently displayed. There is also a large hammer and sickle mounted on the wall. FIDEL CASTRO *sits at his desk. He is accompanied by* CHE GUEVARA *who stands by the doors that open onto the balcony. Mexican Ambassador* GILBERTO BOSQUES *walks in quietly and closes the door behind him.*

FIDEL: Where is she?
BOSQUES: Lía Cámara?
FIDEL: Who else?
CHE: We know she left Cuba on the Mexicana Airlines flight to Mérida yesterday afternoon, Ambassador.
BOSQUES: Yes, she did.
CHE: On a diplomatic passport.
BOSQUES: It's quite natural for a bride-to-be to consult her mother about her wedding plans, isn't it?
FIDEL: On a diplomatic passport? *(Firmly)* Why?
BOSQUES: To make things easier, that's all.
FIDEL: Make things easier? Make what easier?
CHE: *(Menacingly)* Explain, Ambassador.
CHE *and* FIDEL *look at each other.*
BOSQUES: *(Lying, but calmly)* It's not a common occurrence for a Mexican citizen to marry a foreign head of state. *(Pause, looking* FIDEL *directly in the eyes)* When she marries you, Lía Cámara Blum will become Lía Cámara de Castro. And she will become the First Lady of Cuba.
FIDEL: And?
BOSQUES: *(Smiling)* And having a diplomatic passport will allow her to make the transition easier.
CHE: *(Challenging)* Easier?
BOSQUES: Yes, having a diplomatic passport, under

Mexican law, will allow her to become a Cuban citizen without forfeiting her Mexican nationality.

FIDEL *and* CHE *look at each other;* CHE *shrugs his shoulder.*

FIDEL: Very well. *(Pause)* When is she returning?

BOSQUES: My understanding is in a matter of days. *(To reassure the men)* And I'm sure you know her sister arrived this morning.

FIDEL: *(Surprised)* She did?

BOSQUES: She's been invited to give a concert at the Palace of Fine Arts, Comandante Fidel. *(Reassuring)* I'm confident that, having enjoyed her music on so many occasions in the Cámara home in Mérida, you'll welcome the opportunity to hear her play in Havana.

CHE: *(Chuckling)* Bourgeois music's requiem.

FIDEL *gives* CHE *a look.* BOSQUES *clears his throat, unamused by the philistine comment.*

FIDEL: *(To* BOSQUES*)* I'll make a point of attending.

BOSQUES: Excellent, Comandante Fidel!

FIDEL: One more thing, Ambassador.

BOSQUES: Yes?

FIDEL: Let my office know when Lía returns. I want to have my people meet her at the airport.

BOSQUES: Very well.

CHE: *(Walking to* BOSQUES, *invading his personal space)* You're free to go. For now, Ambassador.

BOSQUES *turns to look at* FIDEL *as he opens the door.*

FIDEL: Yes. For now.

BOSQUES: *(Smiling, as he put his fedora on)* I understand, very well, that the last thing Cuba needs is a Comandante with a broken heart.

BOSQUES *exits.* CHE *and* FIDEL *stare at each other in silence.*

CHE: *(With resolve)* I'll have our Consulate in Mérida track her down.

Scene 11

Mérida, Mexico. 1961

The Cámara family residence. Offstage we hear Well Tempered Clavier by Johann Sebastian Bach. LÍA CÁMARA *is gathering her papers—lesson plans—while her father,* PEDRO CÁMARA, *reads the newspaper as the music sounds throughout their living room.* SOCORRO BLUM DE CÁMARA *is heard offstage as the scene opens.*

SOCORRO: *(Offstage)* Lía! You're going to be late!
LÍA: I'm almost ready, Mother.
SOCORRO, *wearing an apron, enters, wiping her hands on a cloth napkin.*
SOCORRO: Your ride is waiting.
PEDRO: *(Looking up from his newspaper)* What's that?
LÍA: That?
PEDRO: *(Pointing to a package on the table)* Yes, that.
LÍA: It's a box of chocolates.
PEDRO: Chocolates?
LÍA: For a friend.
PEDRO: I see.
A car horn is heard.
LÍA: Coming!
SOCORRO: Go! Go!
LÍA *picks up her bag with papers, the package of chocolates, she kisses her father on the head and her mother on the cheek.*
LÍA: Say goodbye to my sister, for me.
PEDRO: We will.
A car horn is heard. She rushes off, looking back at her parents. PEDRO *shakes his head and* SOCORRO *smiles.*
SOCORRO: Go, Lía, go!
SOCORRO *walks to the table, tidies up.* PEDRO *puts the newspaper down, stands, and walks to his wife.*
PEDRO: Chocolates for a friend.

SOCORRO: Yes, I heard.
PEDRO: She's been back six months—and she's still sending chocolates.
SOCORRO: Just be grateful the ambassador was able to help her.
PEDRO: Help her?
SOCORRO: That's his job.
PEDRO: No, no it's not.
SOCORRO: Of course it is! Mexico's ambassador in Cuba there to help Mexican citizens!
PEDRO: Socorro, helping a Mexican citizen who lost her passport is one thing, but helping a Mexican citizen who lost her mind is completely different.
SOCORRO: *(With self-satisfaction)* And let he who has not lost his mind when falling in love cast the first stone!
PEDRO: *(In a huff)* When is she going to find a young man—
SOCORRO:—a young man who's not out there overthrowing governments—
PEDRO:—a doctor would be such a catch.
SOCORRO: God knows she struck out with a lawyer!
PEDRO: Lawyer?
SOCORRO: Fidel. Remember? He has a law degree.
PEDRO: Oh, poor man—
SOCORRO: Do you think the Americans will invade again?
PEDRO: After the Bay of Pigs fiasco?
SOCORRO: Will they?
PEDRO: I don't know, but what I do know is that I'm glad Lía is not in Cuba any longer.

The doorbell rings.

SOCORRO: Who could that be?
PEDRO: I'll get it.

PEDRO *exits.* SOCORRO *business herself tidying up the table.*

PEDRO: *(Offstage)* You won't believe this!
SOCORRO: *(Surprised)* Believe what?
PEDRO *enters. He is holding an envelope.*
PEDRO: It's from the Cubans.
SOCORRO: The Cuban Consulate?

PEDRO: Yes. Again. *(*PEDRO *hands her the envelope, then protesting)* It's for Lía!

SOCORRO: It's always for Lía.

PEDRO *tries to take the letter back, but* SOCORRO *pulls it away.*

SOCORRO: *(She opens it)* I'm just curious.

PEDRO: *(Protesting, but not adamant)* But it's for her!

SOCORRO: She'll get it—but I have a right to know what's going on.

PEDRO: Socorro, she's not a child. *(She gives him a look, a slight pause as* SOCORRO *puts down the cloth napkin and puts on her reading glasses)* What does it say?

SOCORRO: Listen to this.

PEDRO: I'm listening!

SOCORRO: *(Giving him a look)* I was being rhetorical.

PEDRO: Rhetorical?

SOCORRO: Yes, rhetorical!

PEDRO: Well, maybe you should stop being rhetorical and start reading.

SOCORRO: "Lía, the love of my life: Revolution is not a bed of roses. The Yankee Imperialists are determined to destroy the Cuban Revolution. But I am as determined to prevent them from having that satisfaction as long as I live and breathe. My struggle, which is Cuba's struggle, however, would be easier to bear if you were here by my side. History, the history that you taught me and the history of which you reminded me, gives me strength. I find courage in the historic words of José Martí: 'We light the oven so that everyone may bake bread in it.' I fight so that all Cubans may live lives of dignity and social justice. That fight would be more bearable for me with your hand holding mine. For now, the only consolation I have is the satisfaction that I have named a school here in Cuba in your honor. The Escuela Maestra Mexicana Lía Cámara Blum will be a beacon of teaching and understanding, a reminder in Cuba of my love for you that began on that bus ride so long ago. I treasure the chocolates you send me, sweet reminders of our time in Mérida. Only say the word, and the Cuban Consulate is prepared to bring you back to me. Please come back to me. I beg you to come back to me. Your loving Alejandro."

PEDRO: Did José Martí really say, "We light the oven so that everyone may bake bread in it?"

SOCORRO: Yes, he did. He also said, "A selfish man is a thief."

They laugh.

PEDRO: That' a good one! *(Pause)* And the letter?

SOCORRO: What do you mean, the letter?

PEDRO: Are you going to give it to Lía?

SOCORRO: Of course I am! *(Giving him a look)* I can't very well keep it, it's not my letter! It's addressed to her!

SOCORRO *licks the envelope, trying to seal it close again.*

PEDRO: They why did you read it if it's her letter?

SOCORRO: Because I'm her mother—and you didn't stop me?

PEDRO: Oh, so it's my fault you opened it?

SOCORRO: Besides, if you felt that way about it, why didn't you stop me?

PEDRO: Are you being rhetorical?

SOCORRO: What if I am?

PEDRO: Do you think you can seal the letter so she won't know?

SOCORRO: Know what?

PEDRO: That you read the letter, that's what!

SOCORRO: Why are you so argumentative?

PEDRO: I'm not argumentative!

The music beings to fade away as the lights dim. PEDRO *and* SOCORRO *continue to bicker as the lights fade.*

SOCORRO: Of course you are! *(Pause)* If the Cuban exiles in Miami knew how argumentative you were, they'd blame you for Alejandro—

PEDRO:—it's not Alejandro. It's Fidel. Fidel Castro.

SOCORRO: *(Walking to the table and picking up the framed photograph)* Well, they would blame you for Fidel going crazy!

PEDRO: *(Shaking his finger)* Oh, no! Don't you blame me for his going crazy! I just happened to point out that people who are too smart run the risk of going insane!
SOCORRO: Should I throw this photograph out?
PEDRO: Don't.
SOCORRO: Why not?
PEDRO: It's Lía's decision to make.
SOCORRO: But will she?
PEDRO: She will. *(Pause)* When she's good and ready.
SOCORRO: You mean when she no longer loves him. *(Putting the framed photograph down)* Such a wonderful young man, but what a madman he turned out to be. *(Turning to Pedro, in a mocking accusatory manner)* And it's your fault.
PEDRO: My fault?
SOCORRO: Yes, your fault!
PEDRO: I didn't tell him to go nuts! *(Pushing back)* I was *warning* him about going crazy, not *encouraging* him to go crazy.
SOCORRO: Crazy.
PEDRO: Yes, crazy. *(Pause)* Just like that Carlos Torre chess player.
SOCORRO: The chess player?
PEDRO: Yes, the one who's going crazy! The grandmaster who famously sacrificed his queen!
SOCORRO: Going crazy? That chess player isn't going crazy! That chess player is *already* insane?
PEDRO: As insane as the Cuban Revolution, Socorro.
She gives him a look.
SOCORRO: Checkmate!
(They laugh.)

Epilogue

Mérida, Mexico. 2015

It is now 54 years later. The Cámara family residence. The house is now the Escuela de Música Ligia Cámara Blum. Lía's parents and sister—Ligia—have died. LÍA CÁMARA, *now in her 80s, sits at the desk, looking over lesson plans. The color flat screen television is on and there is coverage of the Mexico-Cuba summit taking place a few blocks away. On the screen we see President* RAÚL CASTRO *being welcomed by Mexican President Enrique Peña Nieto.* LÍA *looks up at the live broadcast. The television broadcasts the welcoming ceremonies of this state visit throughout the scene as ambient noise. The doorbell rings as the scene begins.*

LÍA: *(Getting up, walking with a cane)* Coming!
She exits, the television broadcast continues.
LÍA: *(Offstage)* Come in, come in.
She enters with an OFFICIAL *from the Cuban Consulate.*
OFFICIAL: It's not too late.
LÍA: I thank you for the invitation, but I am not feeling well.
OFFICIAL: President Castro asked me to come and invite you once more. He would be honored to have you as his personal guest at the state dinner President Peña Nieto is hosting this evening.
LÍA: *(Shaking her head, as she walks to a chair and sits down. She turns off the television with a remote)* Oh, young man, but so much time has passed! *(Laughing)* What would an old woman like me do at a state dinner?
OFFICIAL: I must ask you once more: Won't you please reconsider and agree to attend?
LÍA: And I must refuse, one final time.
They look at each other.
OFFICIAL: Very well, then. *(Pause)* I have something for you.
LÍA: You do?

OFFICIAL: I was instructed that, if you declined President Castro's invitation to be his personal guest tonight, I was to hand you this letter.

The OFFICIAL reaches into his breast pocket and takes out an envelope. He hands it to her and she takes it. Suddenly, the television begins to broadcast Celia Cruz's version of "Guantanamera," the most patriotic Cuban song, which is played as the Mexican president honors Raúl Castro, is heard softly for the remainder of the scene.

LÍA: *(Smiling)* It's Fidel's handwriting.

OFFICIAL: *(Surprised)* It is?

LÍA: Please give Raúl my regards. *(She looks at the letter, feeling its texture, but she does not open it)* And please close the door on your way out.

The OFFICIAL exits. LÍA CÁMARA stands and, carrying the letter unopened, walks to the table. She places the letter next to the framed photograph taken so many decades ago when she and her mother went to the beach with Alejandro González. She picks up the frame, holds it to her chest, closes her eyes, then kisses the photograph, and puts it back down. She then turns around and walks back to the chair where she was seated. She sits down and returns to her music lesson plans, continuing where she left off. She moves her head softly to the vigor of Celia Cruz's signing, which becomes stronger. The lights go down, except for a single light shining on the framed photograph of Fidel. We hear Celia Cruz's rendition of "Guantanamera" resonating throughout.

FINAL CURTAIN

About Lía Cámara Blum

After returning to Mexico, Lía Cámara Blum married Alberto Sarioli, a Cuban exile.

They had two children and the family moved to Cleveland, Ohio. She could not stand the cold winters and they relocated to Miami, Florida.

The family, however, was not happy in Miami. When members of the Cuban exile community learned of her past there was, almost uniformly, one of three reactions. Most ostracized the family, refusing to have anything to do with them. Others accused her of being a Communist or a spy for Castro, or both. And some were enraged that, having had the opportunity to assassinate Fidel Castro, she had not.

The family returned to Mérida, where Lía Cámara sought to distance herself from her past. Today, a grandmother and a retired teacher, she runs a music school dedicated to her sister's memory, the renowned concert pianist Ligia Cámara.

She has given rare interviews over the decades. It was only after Raúl Castro returned to Mérida for a state visit in November 2015 that she began to share the story of her romance with Fidel. When Teresa Rodríguez of Univision interviewed her, however, she remained circumspect and evasive about her romance with him. A few months later, Fidel Castro died on November 25, 2016. She then authorized the dramatization of her story.

About Fidel Castro

Fidel Castro died November 25, 2016, never seeing Lía Cámara again after she left him.

His tribute to his lost love remains in Cuba: Escuela Maestra Mexicana Lía Cámara Blum.

www.ingramcontent.com/pod-product-compliance
Lightning Source LLC
Chambersburg PA
CBHW022119040426
42450CB00006B/769